The
Only Wise God

The
Only Wise God

**The Compatibility
of Divine Foreknowledge
and Human Freedom**

William Lane Craig

Wipf and Stock Publishers
150 West Broadway • Eugene OR 97401
2000

The Only Wise God:

The Compatibility of Divine Foreknowledge & Human Freedom

By Craig, William Lane
Copyright©1999 by Craig, William Lane

ISBN: 1-57910-316-2

Reprinted by *Wipf and Stock Publishers*
150 West Broadway • Eugene OR 97401

Previously Published by Baker Book House, 1987.

For
Clark and **Ann Peddicord**
liebe Freunde und Geschwister im Herrn

God's foreknowledge has as many
witnesses as he has prophets.
—Tertullian

Contents

PART 3 **The Basis of Divine Foreknowledge**

Preface

This is a book for thinking Christians who would like to understand better the divine attribute of omniscience or who may be troubled over how to reconcile God's foreknowledge with human freedom.

I believe that the philosopher of religion can greatly benefit the body of Christ by helping its members to understand all of God's various attributes, including omniscience. As I read the treatment of divine omniscience in the standard evangelical works of systematic theology, I am often amazed at their superficiality and lack of clear, logical reasoning. I believe that today the Christian seeking after truth will probably learn more about the attributes and nature of God from works of Christian philosophers than from those of Christian theologians. In my own life, I can testify that the philosophical study of divine omniscience, which I have pursued now for several years, has greatly deepened my appreciation of the biblical teaching concerning God's foreknowledge, providence, and infinite wisdom.

Furthermore, modern atheism attacks Christian belief in God not so much because the proofs for God's existence are inadequate, but because it finds the very concept of God unintelligible or incoherent. One attempt to demonstrate incoherence involves the allegation that foreknowledge of future free events is impossible, and thus an omniscient God cannot exist. To cite biblical passages asserting that God does have such foreknowledge does nothing to answer this objection, and

11

Christians may find themselves beset by gnawing doubts even as they affirm the biblical truth. Indeed, there is a disturbing new trend among some evangelical theologians to deny the biblical doctrine of foreknowledge and to explain away scriptural passages asserting this doctrine, simply because the rational attack on it seems to them unanswerable. I hope to show in this book that such an unbiblical concession is altogether unwarranted and that the objection to the truth of divine foreknowledge and human freedom may be rationally resolved.

I have deliberately sought to avoid specialist terminology and to make the arguments as clear and simple as possible. Although the casual reader looking for entertainment or inspiration will probably lack the patience necessary to master the content of this book, I feel certain that any reader who is willing to take the time and make an effort to evaluate the reasoning presented here will find it simple enough to grasp. Readers wishing to go deeper may consult my two forthcoming books *Divine Foreknowledge and Future Contingency from Aristotle to Suárez* (Leiden: E. J. Brill) and *The Coherence of Christian Theism: Omniscience.* The amount of other literature on these subjects is enormous; accordingly, at the end of each chapter I have suggested a few of the very best and most helpful treatments I have discovered.

Most of the research for this book was conducted during sabbaticals at the University of Arizona in Tucson and at the Bibliothèque Nationale in Paris. I am especially indebted to William Asdell for many profitable discussions of the issues handled here. He saved me from many a mistake (any errors that remain, therefore, are just as much his fault as mine). My thanks, too, go to my wife Jan for her typing of the book.

William Lane Craig
Montigny-lès-Cormeilles, France

Introduction

Q*ue sera sera,"* goes the popular song, "whatever will be will be. The future's not ours to see. *Que sera sera.* What will be will be!" Taken literally, these lines express a logical truism. "What will be will be" is true by definition, just like "what has been has been" or "what is, is." To say "what will be will not be" is to utter a self-contradiction. Of course, what will be will be! This is to say nothing more profound or threatening than "what is brown is brown" or "what jumps, jumps."

But of course the words "what will be will be" give us an impression different from their literal meaning. What they seem to suggest is that what will be *must* be. Now that is an entirely different thing! "What will be will be" is just a tautology, but "what will be must be" is an expression of *fatalism.*

According to fatalism, if it is true that something will happen in the future, then it is not within our power to do anything to prevent it. An old Arabic story will serve as an illustration. A man was visiting Damascus and, upon rounding a corner, ran right into the person of Death. Both he and Death were startled to confront each other, and the man, fearing for his life, fled to Jerusalem. The next night Death came to his room and claimed him. "The reason I was startled to see you in Damascus," explained Death, "was that I knew I was to meet you here in Jerusalem tonight, and so I was surprised to find you there!"

Fatalism does not mean that no matter what we do the future would turn out the same. If the man in our story had fled to

13

Baghdad, then he would not have met Death in Jerusalem. But if fatalism is true, the man did not have it within his power to flee to Baghdad or, in fact, to do anything other than what he did do. Fatalism is thus a denial of human freedom. It entails that, if we shall act in a certain way, then we are not free to act in a different way. Whatever we shall do, we must do. Fatalism, if true, is threatening, since there is nothing we can do to avoid our fate.

Now fatalism should not be confused with determinism, the view that all our choices and actions are determined by prior causes. Given a series of causes up to some point, the effect at that point is completely predetermined. There is at that point no freedom to act in another way, for, given the prior series of causes, one's choice is causally necessary; that is to say, the causes determine one's choice. By contrast, fatalism does not necessarily hold that everything is causally determined. A fatalist could hold that a prior series of causes does not completely determine what we shall choose at a certain point and yet that it is still not within our power to choose anything other than what we shall choose. Fatalism does not appeal to causal factors to deny human freedom; rather it holds that from the very fact that we *shall* do some action, we *must* do that action. If it is now true, for example, that on April 1 of next year I shall eat pizza, then when April 1 arrives I *must* eat pizza, and I am not free to do anything else, even if my action is not at that point causally determined.

At this point the reader may be thinking that such a view is so weird and abstract that it is not worth one's time to refute it, much less to write a book about it. But in fact fatalism and fatalistic reasoning, although usually not recognized as such, can be shown to be very widespread. Historically, fatalism dominated the thinking of ancient Greece, and the early church fathers had to argue strenuously against it to support the concept of human freedom. More recently, the Oxford philosopher Michael A. E. Dummett reminisces that during the Second World War in the dark days of the Battle of Britain, when Nazi missiles and bombs pounded London nightly, many people lost their lives because they refused to take refuge in the bomb shelters. They reasoned, "If I am going to be killed, then I am going to be killed, whether or not I take precautions. And if I am going to live, then I am going to live, whether or not I take precautions.

Since I am either going to be killed or going to live, why bother taking precautions?"

Theologically, too, fatalism has been very influential. It was readily obvious to the church fathers (and to pagan philosophers as well) that the Greek argument for fatalism could be very easily cast in a theological form by referring to God's foreknowledge: if God foreknows that something will happen at a certain time, then when that time arrives, the event *must* happen; otherwise, God's foreknowledge could be mistaken, a notion which was theologically unacceptable. The church fathers and medieval theologians sought to refute such theological fatalism, but some later theologians willingly embraced it. The great Protestant Reformer Martin Luther, for example, argued that given an omnipotent and omniscient God who foreknows our every thought, it is impossible that we should do anything other than what we in fact do; freedom to do otherwise is an illusion. Certain Calvinist theologians, notably the brilliant American theologian and revivalist Jonathan Edwards, argued similarly. In our own day Paul Helm, a Calvinist philosopher of religion, has repeatedly and vigorously defended theological fatalism.

By contrast, certain other evangelical theologians, repelled by theological fatalism but apparently unable to find any flaw in the fatalist's reasoning, have been led to repudiate divine foreknowledge as a result. In so doing, they seem to be following the lead of process theologians who, as part of their general denial of God's perfection in favor of the concept of a gradually improving God, have rejected divine foreknowledge. For the Christian, then, the issue of fatalism—more particularly, theological fatalism—cannot remain a matter of indifference. If the fatalist is correct, then the Christian must deny either divine foreknowledge or human freedom.

The problem cannot be convincingly sidestepped by appeals to divine mystery. When my wife Jan and I were studying in Cambridge, England, we stopped in at the local Christian bookstore. When the saleswoman asked the subject of my research, I explained that I was studying the compatibility of divine foreknowledge and human freedom. "Oh, well," she replied with a smile, "we can't really know the answer to that, can we?" For too many Christians, easy appeal to mystery has become a substitute for the labor of hard thinking. But such an appeal is of little use against Christian theologians who are fatalists, and it will hardly convince non-Christian philosophers who, on the basis of theological fatalism, reject as unintelligible the Christian concept of God. This is not to say that theology has no place for mystery, but that such an appeal ought to be made only as a last resort after much hard thinking. Indeed, with regard to the problem of theological fatalism, I think we shall see that the saleslady was wrong: we can, without appealing to mystery, show the compatibility of divine foreknowledge and human freedom.

Our inquiry into this problem shall be divided into three parts. In part 1 we shall examine the biblical doctrine of divine foreknowledge of future free decisions. I shall argue that the Bible teaches divine foreknowledge of human free acts and that attempts to deny this doctrine either cannot account convincingly for all the various scriptural references to God's foreknowledge or else wind up making God the author of sin.

Then in part 2 we shall examine the arguments for theological fatalism, with a view toward showing the compatibility of divine foreknowledge and human freedom. After laying out the basic argument for theological fatalism (chap. 3), I shall try to show that three proposed escape routes from fatalism—namely, denying that future-tense statements are either true or false, holding that all future-tense statements are false, and maintaining that God's knowledge is timeless—are ultimately unsuccessful (chap. 4). I shall contend, rather, that the whole idea of fatalism is incoherent and that the fatalistic argument commits a logical fallacy. It infers from God's foreknowledge of some future event that that event *must* happen, when all one has the right to conclude is that the event *will* happen (chap. 5). Some fatalists try to correct this fallacy by making God's foreknowledge necessary in some sense, but I shall argue that no fatalist has ever explained the necessity at issue as anything other than the impossibility of changing the past or the impossibility of backward causation, neither of which imposes necessity on the content of God's foreknowledge (chap. 6). I shall then show how fatalistic reasoning has been rejected in areas other than theology, thereby confirming my contention that it should be rejected in theology too (chaps. 7–10).

In part 3 we shall address the question of how God foreknows future events which are not causally determined. There are at least two possibilities. One could hold that God simply possesses innate knowledge of all truth, including truth about future free acts. Or one could subscribe to a doctrine of divine middle knowledge. According to this second possibility, in the moment logically prior to the decree to create the world, God knew what everyone would freely do under any circumstances. And so by decreeing to place certain persons in certain circumstances, he knows what they will freely do. In the end, I think we shall see that the biblical conceptions of God as perfectly omniscient and of human beings as genuinely free are entirely compatible notions. The philosophical study of this question shall, I trust, deepen our appreciation of the biblical truth in this regard.

PART 1

The Doctrine
of Divine Foreknowledge

God's Knowledge of the Present, Past, and Future

The LORD is a God of knowledge," sings Hannah in praise to God (1 Sam. 2:3), and what a God of knowledge he is! Isaiah declares that "his understanding is unsearchable" (Isa. 40:28), and the psalmist similarly proclaims that "his understanding is beyond measure" (Ps. 147:5). Both the prophet and the psalmist thereby indicate that the depth of God's knowledge is inexhaustible and limitless. In the same way, the psalmist ponders the infinite extent of God's knowledge, singing,

> How precious to me are thy thoughts, O God!
>   How vast is the sum of them!
> If I would count them, they are more than the sand.
>   When I awake, I am still with thee.
>
> [Ps. 139:17–18]

No finite number can serve to enumerate what God knows; his knowledge is infinite. The sense of the final line of verse 18 is that it is impossible to come to the end of God's knowledge. No matter how far the psalmist should count, even should he fall asleep wearied from his meditation, still, upon his awaking, the infinite expanse of God's knowledge would stretch away before him.

21

God's Knowledge of the Present

Taken in isolation, the assertions of the prophet and psalmist might be interpreted as religious hyperbole; but the Old and New Testaments consistently portray God as the one who knows everything, including all things present, past, and future. With regard to things present, nothing escapes the knowledge of God, who is often described as observing everything that goes on in his creation: "For he looks to the ends of the earth, and sees everything under the heavens" (Job 28:24). His knowledge ranges from the greatest to the most insignificant aspects of creation. On the one hand, he knows the number and nature of the stars (Ps. 147:4; Job 38:31–33; Isa. 40:26). On the other hand, Jesus taught that not a single sparrow dies without God's knowledge and that the very hairs of our heads are numbered (Matt. 10:29–30).

But God does not merely observe what goes on in the created order; he *understands* it. God's answer to Job out of the whirlwind (Job 38–41) is a magnificent description of God's knowledge of the creation's profoundest secrets. "Who is this that darkens counsel by words without knowledge?" the Lord challenges Job, and then he proceeds to interrogate him concerning the wonders of the universe. Does Job understand the origin and expanse of the world, has he penetrated to the deepest recesses of the sea, does he know the laws that regulate the stars and the heavens, does he comprehend birth and death, does he have the intelligence to govern the magnificent animal kingdom? Job's mouth is stopped; he can only answer, "I have uttered what I did not understand, things too wonderful for me, which I did not know" (Job 42:3). In contrast to human ignorance, God's wisdom and understanding encompass the entire created order (Job 28:12–27).

God's knowledge of creation includes knowledge of all human affairs:

> The LORD looks down from heaven,
>   he sees all the sons of men;
> from where he sits enthroned he looks forth
>   on all the inhabitants of the earth,
> he who fashions the hearts of them all,
>   and observes all their deeds.

> [Ps. 33:13–15]

The Scriptures repeatedly tell us that God's eyes observe all the ways and acts of an individual (Job 24:23; 31:4; 34:21; Ps. 119:168; Jer. 16:17; 32:19; cf. Ps. 14:2; 2 Chron. 16:9).

God does not, however, observe merely our *actions*, but in one of the most startling affirmations of divine omniscience, we are told that God knows our very *thoughts*. One of Jeremiah's characteristic emphases, for example, is that God discerns and weighs human hearts and minds:

> The heart is deceitful above all things,
>   and desperately corrupt;
>   who can understand it?
> "I the LORD search the mind
>   and try the heart,
> to give to every man according to his ways,
>   according to the fruit of his doings."
>
> [Jer. 17:9–10]

In the Hebrew idiom the heart denotes the center of the human personality in all its spiritual, intellectual, emotional, and ethical aspects. That God knows even this inner sanctum of human beings is a characteristic theme in Old Testament religion. The Lord says to Samuel, "The LORD sees not as man sees; man looks on the outward appearance, but the LORD looks on the heart" (1 Sam. 16:7). David instructs Solomon that "the LORD searches all hearts, and understands every plan and thought" (1 Chron. 28:9). Solomon prays, "Render to each whose heart thou knowest, according to all his ways (for thou, thou only, knowest the hearts of all the children of men)" (1 Kings 8:39). Sins concealed in the heart separate us from God. Therefore, we are to pray,

> Search me, O God, and know my heart!
> Try me and know my thoughts!
> And see if there be any wicked way in me,
>   and lead me in the way everlasting!
>
> [Ps. 139:23–24; cf. Pss. 7:9; 94:11][1]

---

1. Psalm 139 also suggests that God knows the realm of the dead (vv. 7–8; cf. Amos 9:2). So also Job 26:5–6: "The shades below tremble, / the waters and their inhabitants. / Sheol is naked before God, / and Abaddon has no cov-

Note that the metaphor of sight extends to God's knowledge of human hearts and thoughts: God "seest the heart and the mind" and so judges us (Jer. 20:12). Even as nothing happening in the physical world escapes his notice, so no secret thought or inner motive remains unknown to him. As Jesus warned the self-righteous Pharisees, "God knows your hearts" (Luke 16:15).

The New Testament likewise insists on God's knowledge of the heart (Acts 1:24; 15:8; Rom. 8:27; 1 Cor. 4:5; 1 John 3:19–20). The writer of the Epistle to the Hebrews splendidly summarizes the biblical conviction concerning God's intimate knowledge of our inner thoughts:

> For the word of God is living and active, sharper than any two-edged sword, piercing to the division of soul and spirit, of joints and marrow, and discerning the thoughts and intentions of the heart. And before him no creature is hidden, but all are open and laid bare to the eyes of him with whom we have to do. [Heb. 4:12–13]

Thus the minds of individuals as well as their actions lie naked before the all-knowing God.

God's Knowledge of the Past

If God so knows the present, it scarcely needs to be said that God also knows completely the past. He is eternal and created the universe by his wisdom (Ps. 90:2; Prov. 8:22–31). Since every moment of the past was once present and God knows all things happening in the present, the only way in which his knowledge of the past might be incomplete would be for him to forget something. But such a lapse of memory is foreign to the biblical God. One finds little reference to God's memory in the Scriptures simply because the notion of his having known

---

ering." A shade is the Hebrew equivalent of the Greek notion of a disembodied soul (see Robert Gundry, *Sōma in Biblical Theology* [Cambridge: Cambridge University Press, 1974], pp. 117–34). In knowing the nether realms, God knows the minds of disembodied persons. If he knows the realm of the shades, what difficulty is there in knowing our thoughts? "Sheol and Abaddon lie open before the LORD, / how much more the hearts of men!" (Prov. 15:11).

something but then forgotten it is inconceivable. True, he is said to remember no longer the sins of those who turn to him in repentance and faith (Isa. 43:25; Jer. 31:34), but this is clearly a reference to his forgiving sins, not to a literal extinguishing of memory on God's part. Indeed, when the concepts of remembering and forgetting are used with respect to God, they usually have to do with the notion of God's faithfulness to his people or covenant (Exod. 2:24; Deut. 4:31; Ps. 98:3) and the faithlessness of Israel to God (1 Sam. 12:9; Isa. 17:10; Jer. 2:32; Hos. 4:6). God remembers his people, though they consistently forget him. When prayers are offered that God remember some deed of the wicked and exact vengeance or remember some affliction and bring comfort, the petition is not that he merely retain some fact, but that he make and keep it an object of concern. It is in this sense that Jesus says that the fifth sparrow thrown in for the price of four is not forgotten before God (Luke 12:6).

Of course, to maintain something as an object of concern, one must remember it, and the Scriptures have no doubt about God's mental capacity in this regard. Job says that God numbers all his steps (Job 31:4). The psalmist in affliction comforts himself by praying,

> Thou hast kept count of my tossings;
> put thou my tears in thy bottle!
> Are they not in thy book?

> [Ps. 56:8]

God has, as it were, a book of remembrance (Mal. 3:16) in which every tossing and tear of his afflicted servant is recorded. Of course, the language is poetical, but the Scriptures implicitly assume that just as God sees everything that happens, he remembers everything that has happened and every fact that he has known.

God's Knowledge of the Future

The Importance of Divine Foreknowledge

Finally, it would seem, at least at face value, that God possesses complete knowledge of every future event. This aspect of divine omniscience seems to underlie the biblical scheme of history. For the biblical conception of history is not that of an unpredictably unfolding sequence of events plunging haphazardly without purpose or direction; rather God knows the future and directs the course of world history toward his foreseen ends.

> I am God, and there is none like me,
> declaring the end from the beginning
>   and from ancient times things not yet done,
> saying, "My counsel shall stand,
>   and I will accomplish all my purpose."
>
> [Isa. 46:9–10]

Again Isaiah proclaims,

> Thus says the LORD, the King of Israel
>   and his Redeemer, the LORD of hosts:
> "I am the first and I am the last;
>   besides me there is no god.
> Who is like me? Let him proclaim it,
>   let him declare and set it forth before me.
> Who has announced from of old the things to come?
>   Let them tell us what is yet to be.
> Fear not, nor be afraid;
>   have I not told you from of old and declared it?
>   And you are my witnesses!
> Is there a God besides me?
>   There is no Rock; I know not any."
>
> [Isa. 44:6–8]

In the vision of the apostle John in the Book of Revelation, some of these same words are ascribed to the exalted Christ: "Fear not, I am the first and the last"; "I am the Alpha and the Omega, the first and the last, the beginning and the end" (Rev. 1:17; 22:13). Biblical history is a salvation history, and Christ is the beginning, centerpiece, and culmination of that history. God's salvific plan was not an afterthought necessitated by an unforeseen circumstance. Paul speaks of "the plan of the mystery hidden for ages in God who created all things," "a plan for the fulness of time" according to "the eternal purpose which he has realized in

Christ Jesus our Lord" (Eph. 3:9; 1:10; 3:11; cf. 2 Tim. 1:9–10). Similarly, Peter states that Christ "was destined before the foundation of the world but was made manifest at the end of the times for your sake" (1 Peter 1:20). God's knowledge of the course of world history and his control over it to achieve his purposes seem fundamental to the biblical conception of history and are a source of comfort and assurance to the believer in times of distress.

Moreover, God's knowledge of the future seems essential to the prophetic pattern that underlies the biblical scheme of history. The test of the true prophet was success in foretelling the future: "When a prophet speaks in the name of the LORD, if the word does not come to pass or come true, that is a word which the LORD has not spoken" (Deut. 18:22). The history of Israel was punctuated with prophets who foretold events in both the immediate and distant future, and it was the conviction of the New Testament writers that the coming and work of Jesus had been prophesied. God foretold to Abraham the four-hundred-year captivity and the exodus of the Hebrew people (Gen. 15:13–14). Joseph claimed from God the power to interpret dreams which presaged the future (Gen. 40:8). He was able to predict Pharaoh's restoration of his chief butler and his execution of his chief baker, as well as the seven years of plenty and seven years of famine that Egypt would experience. God told Moses that after their deliverance from Egypt his people would forsake him and worship foreign deities, so that God would visit his wrath upon them (Deut. 31:16–17).

During the days of the divided kingdom, an unnamed prophet from Judah predicted the birth of King Josiah and his destruction of pagan religious practices in Israel, and he gave as a sign of his authenticity the prediction that the altar would soon be destroyed (1 Kings 13:2–3). When this same prophet disobeyed God, his own imminent death was prophesied by another prophet, and before he could return to Judah he was attacked and killed by a lion (1 Kings 13:20–24). Elisha prophesied the death of the king of Syria, as well as the terrible reign of his successor (2 Kings 8:7–15). Amos and Hosea prophesied the fall of the northern kingdom of Israel. Isaiah, Jeremiah, and Ezekiel foretold the fall of the southern kingdom of Judah and the destruction of Jerusalem, the Babylonian captivity, and the restoration

of Israel, as well as the doom of Assyria, Babylon, and many
lesser nations. Daniel predicted the three successive empires to
follow the Babylonian Empire (Dan. 2:36–43) and the course of
world history from the Persian Empire well into the intertesta-
mental period (Dan. 11).

Our basic concern here is not whether these prophecies are in
fact genuine predictions rather than inferences from current
events or retrojections actually written after the fact or just
religious folklore, as some biblical critics might claim; rather
the point is that the conception of God presupposed throughout
the Old Testament seems to be that of a God who foreknows the
future and can disclose it to his prophets. For these prophecies
are represented as divine disclosures of what will take place.
Not human perceptiveness, but the "word of the LORD" or "the
Spirit of the LORD" enables the prophet to foretell future events.
Whatever we make of the claim to prophesy the future, it is clear
that the theology of the Old Testament represents prophecy as a
gift of God, who discloses the future.

The New Testament continues the prophetic pattern of the
Old. The writers of the New Testament are persuaded that Old
Testament prophecies pointed forward to Jesus as their fulfilment. As Peter says, "The prophets who prophesied of the grace
that was to be yours searched and inquired about this salvation;
they inquired what person or time was indicated by the Spirit of
Christ within them when predicting the sufferings of Christ and
the subsequent glory" (1 Peter 1:10–11). That Jesus himself held
this conviction is evident in his upbraiding the Emmaus disciples, "'O foolish men, and slow of heart to believe all that the
prophets have spoken! Was it not necessary that the Christ
should suffer these things and enter into his glory?' And beginning with Moses and all the prophets, he interpreted to them in
all the scriptures the things concerning himself" (Luke
24:25–27; cf. vv. 45–47). The Gospel writers are at pains to
point out where in the life and ministry of Jesus Old Testament
prophecies were fulfilled (Matt. 1:22; 2:15, 23; 4:14–16; 8:17;
12:17–21; Mark 1:2–4; 9:9–13; Luke 7:18–23, 27; 18:31–33;
Acts 2:16–21; 3:18; 4:25–28; 7:52; 8:30–35; 10:43; 15:15–18;
John 12:38–41; 19:24, 28, 36).

The prophetic element, however, is not limited to the fulfilment of Old Testament predictions. Jesus himself is char-

acterized as a prophet, and he predicts the destruction of Jerusalem, signs of the end of the world, and his own return as Lord of all nations (Matt. 24; Mark 13; Luke 21). In the early church, too, there were prophets who told of events to come (Acts 11:27–28; 21:10–11; see also 13:1; 15:32; 21:9; 1 Cor. 12:28–29; 14:29, 37; Eph. 4:11). The Revelation to John is a mighty vision of the end of human history: "The Lord, the God of the spirits of the prophets, has sent his angel to show his servants what must soon take place" (Rev. 22:6). The prophetic pattern thus reveals an underlying unity, not only between the two Testaments, but beneath the entire course of human history.

The biblical view of history and prophecy thus seems to necessitate a God who knows not only the present and past, but also the future. Indeed, so essential is God's knowledge of the future that Isaiah makes knowledge of the future the decisive test in distinguishing the true God from false gods. The prophet flings this challenge in the teeth of all pretenders to deity:

> Set forth your case, says the LORD;
>   bring your proofs, says the King of Jacob.
> Let them bring them, and tell us
>   what is to happen.
> Tell us the former things, what they are,
>   that we may consider them,
> that we may know their outcome;
>   or declare to us the things to come.
> Tell us what is to come hereafter,
>   that we may know that you are gods;
> do good, or do harm,
>   that we may be dismayed and terrified.
> Behold, you are nothing,
>   and your work is nought;
>   an abomination is he who chooses you.

> [Isa. 41:21–24]

Stephen Charnock in his classic *Existence and Attributes of God* comments on this passage:

Such a foreknowledge of things to come is here ascribed to God by God himself, as a distinction of him from all false gods. Such a knowledge that, if any could prove that they were possessors of, he would acknowledge them as gods as well as himself: "that we may know that you are gods." He puts his Deity to stand or fall upon this account, and this should be the point which should decide the controversy whether he or the heathen idols were the true God. The dispute is managed by this medium: he that knows things to come is God; I know things to come, *ergo* I am God: the idols know not things to come, therefore they are not gods. God submits the being of his Deity to this trial. If God knows things to come no more than the heathen idols, which were either devils or men, he would be, in his own account, no more a God than devils or men. . . . It cannot be understood of future things in their causes, when the effects necessarily arise from such causes, as light from the sun and heat from the fire. Many of these men know; more of them, angels and devils know; if God, therefore, had not a higher and farther knowledge than this, he would not by this be proved to be God, any more than angels and devils, who know necessary effects in their causes. The devils, indeed, did predict some things in the heathen oracles, but God is differenced from them here . . . in being able to predict things to come that they knew not, or things in their particularities, things that depended on the liberty of man's will, which the devils could lay no claim to a certain knowledge of. Were it only a conjectural knowledge that is here meant, the devils might answer they can conjecture, and so their deity were as good as God's. . . . God asserts his knowledge of things to come as a manifest evidence of his Godhead; those that deny, therefore, the argument that proves it, deny the conclusion, too; for this will necessarily follow, that if he be God because he knows future things, then he that doth not know future things is not God; and if God knows not future things but only by conjecture, then there is no God, because a certain knowledge, so as infallibly to predict things to come, is an inseparable perfection of the Deity.[2]

Thus the God of Israel was conceived to possess foreknowledge of the future, a property which distinguished him from all false gods.

The Old Testament Doctrine of Foreknowledge

As Charnock notes, God's knowledge seems to encompass future contingencies: God foreknows the results of Nebuchad-

---

2. Stephen Charnock, *The Existence and Attributes of God* (1682; reprint, Grand Rapids: Baker, 1979), vol. 1, pp. 431–32.

nezzar's divinations to determine his battle routes (Ezek. 21:21–23). Even more remarkably, just as God knows the thoughts humans have, so he foreknows the very thoughts they will have. The psalmist declares,

> O LORD, thou hast searched me and known me!
> Thou knowest when I sit down and when I rise up;
>   thou discernest my thoughts from afar.
> Thou searchest out my path and my lying down,
>   and art acquainted with all my ways.
> Even before a word is on my tongue,
>   lo, O LORD, thou knowest it altogether.
> Thou dost beset me behind and before,
>   and layest thy hand upon me.
> Such knowledge is too wonderful for me;
>   it is high, I cannot attain it.
>
> [Ps. 139:1–6]

Here the psalmist envisages himself as surrounded by God's knowledge. God knows everything about him, even his thoughts. "From afar" *(mērāḥôq)* may be taken to indicate temporal distance—God knows the psalmist's thoughts long before he thinks them. Similarly, even before he speaks a word, God knows what he will say. Little wonder that such knowledge is beyond the reach of the psalmist's understanding! But such is the knowledge of Israel's God in contradistinction to all the false gods of her neighbors.

The New Testament Doctrine of Foreknowledge

Technical terminology

One of the contributions of the New Testament to the doctrine of foreknowledge is its bringing in a family of words associated with God's knowledge of the future, such as "foreknow" *(proginōskō)*, "foreknowledge" *(prognōsis)*, "foresee" *(prooraō)*, "foreordain" *(proorizō)*, and "foretell" *(promarturomai, prokatangellō)*. In certain cases, *proginōskō* and *prooraō* mean simply that one has known or seen (someone or something) previously. For example, in Acts 26:5 Paul states that the Jews had previously known for a long time the strictness of his life as a Pharisee, and in Acts 21:29 Luke mentions that the Jews had previously seen *(proorao)* Trophimus in Paul's company. This sense is probably operative in Romans 11:2 as well, where Paul states of apostate Israel that "God has not rejected his people whom he foreknew [*proginōskō*]," that is, whom he had previously known in an intimate way.[3] Similarly, when Peter warns his readers of the danger posed by heretics' twisting the Scriptures, he commands them, "You therefore, beloved, knowing this beforehand [*proginōskō*], beware. . ." (2 Peter 3:17). What they know is not the future, but some present danger which might possibly confront them in the future as well. *Proorao* can, in addition to the temporal meaning, have the sense of "to see up ahead," as in Acts 2:25 ("I saw the Lord always before me"), though here, as we shall soon note, there does seem to be a double meaning, Peter playing upon the ambiguity of *proorao* to suggest seeing the future as well.

In other cases, however, the *pro-* words clearly refer to actual fore-knowledge, -sight, -ordination, or -telling. For example, we have seen that according to Peter the Old Testament prophets by the Spirit of Christ foretold *(promarturomai)* the sufferings and exaltation of Christ (1 Peter 1:11). Similarly, in Peter's second sermon in Acts we find, "But what God foretold [*prokatangellō*] by the mouth of all the prophets, that his Christ should suffer, he thus fulfilled" (Acts 3:18); and again in Stephen's speech, "Which of the prophets did not your fathers persecute? And they killed those who announced beforehand [*prokatangellō*] the coming of the Righteous One" (Acts 7:52). The prophet's ability to foretell the future is rooted in God's foresight or foreknowledge. Paul states, "The scripture, foreseeing that God would justify the Gentiles by faith, preached the gospel beforehand [*proeuangelizomai*] to Abraham, saying, 'In you shall all the nations be blessed'" (Gal. 3:8). Of course, the Scripture itself did not say this to Abraham, but God did, and Scripture records the fact; nor does the Scripture foresee the future, but the God who inspired the Scripture does. Paul's meaning, then, is that God,

---

3. It seems unlikely that Paul means "whom God knew intimately in advance," because the object of foreknowledge here is not the elect but the unbelieving Jews. On the unlikelihood of "foreknow" meaning "choose in advance," see p. 34.

foreseeing that he would justify the Gentiles by faith, preached the gospel of justification by faith to Abraham in advance.

Both God's foresight and foreknowledge are referred to in Luke's rendition of Peter's sermon on Pentecost. Peter proclaims, "This Jesus, delivered up according to the definite plan and foreknowledge of God, you crucified and killed by the hands of lawless men" (Acts 2:23). Then citing Psalm 16:8–11, in which David says, "I saw the Lord always before me [*prooraō*]," Peter comments, "Being therefore a prophet, . . . he foresaw [*prooraō*] and spoke of the resurrection of the Christ" (Acts 2:25, 30–31). The meaning of verse 23 seems to be that Jesus' being handed over was not accidental or unexpected but was in accord with God's decided purpose and foreknowledge of what would happen. This interpretation is reinforced by the wordplay on David's foreseeing the Lord, which is taken to apply to his foreseeing Messiah's resurrection.

A similar thought is expressed in 1 Peter 1:19–20, where he explains that we have been redeemed "by the precious blood. . . of Christ, foreknown [*proginōskō*] before the foundation of the world but revealed in the last times for your sake" (my translation). *Proginōskō* in 1 Peter 1:19–20 is often taken to mean "predestine," but it is noteworthy that Peter does not use *proorizō* here, which could convey that meaning, but *proginōskō*, which means simply "foreknow." Although one could substitute "foreordain" for "foreknow" in verse 20 and still make perfect sense, that does not prove that the meaning of the sentence would not thereby be changed. The fact is, there is simply no linguistic evidence, biblical or extrabiblical, that these words can be used as synonyms.

We should point out, however, that in Acts 4:28 Luke does speak in terms reminiscent of 2:23—Herod and Pilate, together with the Gentiles and Jews, were gathered together against Jesus "to do whatever your hand and your plan foreordained [*proorizō*] to happen" (my translation). But from these passages we cannot be sure that foreknowledge is based on foreordination rather than the reverse. Could not God's foreordination be based on his knowledge of what Herod, Pilate, and the others would do should Christ be sent? Technically, this is not foreknowledge, but so-called middle knowledge, which we shall discuss in chapter 12; that is to say, it is *prognōsis* in the sense that God knew in advance what would happen were he to send his Son. For the moment, however, the essential point is that foreknowledge and foreordination do not mean the same thing, and the latter could be based on the former rather than the other way around.

Foreknowledge of God's elect is a more complex issue. There are two key references in the New Testament:

> Peter, an apostle of Jesus Christ, to the chosen ones . . . according to the foreknowledge of God the Father. . . . [1 Peter 1:1–2, my translation]

> For whom he foreknew, he also foreordained to be conformed to the image of his Son. . . . [Rom. 8:29, my translation]

Here the meaning of "foreknow" cannot be reduced without redundancy to "foreordain," since Peter has already referred to his readers as chosen or elect, while Paul uses "foreordain" as a consequence of "foreknow." It is sometimes suggested that "foreknow" with regard to the elect means "choose in advance," so that foreknowledge and unconditional election to salvation become synonymous. But again there is no linguistic evidence in support of this suggestion. Out of the 770 cases of *yāda'* ("to know") in the Old Testament, the 660 instances of *ginōskō* ("to know") in the Septuagint, and the 220 in the New Testament, the term never carries the sense of "choose" or "elect."[4] In the references usually adduced in support of this meaning (Amos 3:2; Hos. 13:5; Gen. 18:19; Jer. 1:5; 1 Cor. 8:3; Gal. 4:9), the more natural sense of the word is "to know personally and intimately" or "to acknowledge." Now it needs to be asked whether this might not be the meaning in 1 Peter 1:1–2 and Romans 8:29—that God foreknows his elect in the sense that he personally knows them in advance. On the basis of his personally knowing certain individuals, before they come to be, God elects them and foreordains them to glorification. I think we have to allow that this is a plausible interpretation of "foreknow" in these passages. But even if we construe foreknowledge in this personal sense, we are still presupposing that God "foreknows"

---

4. See the word study by Roger T. Forster and V. Paul Marston, *God's Strategy in Human History* (Wheaton, Ill.: Tyndale, 1973), pp. 179–90.

in the more intellectual sense of the term the range of future individuals from which he knows intimately those he then elects.[5]

Christ's foreknowledge

A second contribution of the New Testament concerning foreknowledge is its attribution of such knowledge to Christ himself. Obviously Jesus in his preresurrection state did not consciously know all things. Not only is this implied in his intercourse with people and events, but it was admitted by him with regard to the date of his second coming (Mark 13:32). Nevertheless, all the Gospels represent Jesus as possessing foreknowledge of various future events. In Matthew, Mark, and Luke, he foretells his passion, death, and resurrection (Mark 8:31; 9:31; 10:32–34, and parallels). In order to pay the temple tax, he commands Peter to "go to the sea and cast a hook, and take the first fish that comes up, and when you open its mouth you will find a shekel; take that and give it to them for me and for yourself" (Matt. 17:27).[6] In Mark 13 and 14 Jesus exhibits an amazing knowledge of future events both imminent and distant. When his disciples ask about the times and signs of the destruction of the temple, an event which he had predicted, Jesus expounds at length in his Olivet discourse the course of the last days prior to his return (Mark 13 and parallels; see also Luke 17:22–37). In arranging to celebrate his final Passover, Jesus commands two of his disciples, "Go into the city, and a man carrying a jar of water will meet you; follow him, and wherever he enters, say to the householder, 'The Teacher says, Where is my guest room, where I am to eat the passover with my disciples?' And he will show you a large upper room furnished

---

5. This conclusion would not follow, however, if we regard election as corporate rather than individual. For then the object of foreknowledge and election would be the body of Christ in general. For a view of corporate election, see the readable treatment by Robert Shank, *Elect in the Son* (Springfield, Mo.: Westcott, 1970); see also Forster and Marston, *God's Strategy*.

6. This remarkable prediction might better be classed as an example of middle knowledge on Jesus' part. Or the incident could be taken to be a miracle of telekinesis, though this would still involve clairvoyance on Jesus' part. There is no suggestion, however, that Jesus makes the fish come up; the event seems entirely contingent.

and ready; there prepare for us" (Mark 14:13–15). The prediction concerning the water carrier is remarkable not merely because it deals with a free event, but also because in first-century Palestine only women carried jars of water (some critics have accordingly regarded this detail as a historical error on Mark's part).[7] Hence Jesus is here represented as foreknowing a free and highly singular event. During the Passover meal, Jesus foretells his betrayal by Judas (Mark 14:18–20 and parallels). Then after the supper, he predicts the disciples' abandoning him and the threefold denial of Peter (Mark 14:27–30 and parallels)—predictions which are soon tragically fulfilled.

To suggest that these last predictions were not founded on foreknowledge, but were inferences based on the character of the disciples and the context of events soon to occur, is to evacuate the incidents of all theological significance whatever. These events were remembered by the early church because they taught something about the Lord, namely, his mastery over and full awareness of all he was to undergo; but if these predictions were just inferences, then Jesus' giving them is devoid of significance. Again, our focus is not on whether Jesus actually gave true prophecies of the future; rather, the point is that he is represented as possessing the same sort of foreknowledge as is ascribed in the Old Testament to God. The theology of the first three Gospels clearly presents Jesus as foreknowing events which were beyond the capacity of any human inference. It was this claim to superhuman knowledge which was the butt of the Jews' cruel mockery at Jesus' trial when they blindfolded him, struck him in the face, and cried, "Prophesy to us, you Christ! Who is it that struck you?" (Matt. 26:68).

The Gospel of John also portrays Jesus as foreknowing future events. John seems to underline Jesus' clairvoyant and precognitive knowledge. Nathanael believes in Christ because of Jesus' knowledge of him without any personal contact (John 1:47–50). Knowing what is in people who believe in him because of his miracles, Jesus does not trust himself to them (2:24–25). Jesus tells Nicodemus that the Son of man possesses knowledge of heavenly as well as earthly things (3:10–12). He is able to dis-

---

7. E.g., Pierson Parker, "A Second Look at *The Gospel Before Mark*," *Journal of Biblical Literature* 100 (1981): 396.

close the private life of a woman of Samaria whom he had never met before (4:17–19, 29). Some of his questions to the disciples are merely to test them, for he already knows the answer (6:6). He knows who among his followers do not truly believe in him, and he knows who will betray him (6:64). Jesus knows his heavenly origin and his eventual return to God through death and resurrection (7:33; 8:14, 21–28; 12:32–33; 13:3). The stories of Jesus' predictions of Judas's betrayal and Peter's threefold denial are narrated (13:21–27, 36–38). Jesus predicts the immediate scattering of his disciples (16:32) and their later expulsion from the synagogues (16:1–4). John emphasizes that Jesus foretells such things so that when his predictions are fulfilled, the disciples may be confirmed in their faith (13:19; 14:29; 16:4; see also 2:22). In John's mind Jesus' supernatural knowledge is an unmistakable sign of his divine origin and mission.

Thus, in the New Testament as well as the Old, God is conceived as knowing not only all present and past events, but all future events as well. This foreknowledge would seem to extend to future free acts, events which could not possibly be inferred from present causes and which in any case are not so represented by the biblical authors. We have seen examples throughout Scripture of God's foreknowledge of such events, including even the thoughts which individuals shall have. It does not, therefore, seem possible to deny that the biblical conception of God's omniscience includes foreknowledge of future free acts.

Suggested Further Reading

Charnock, Stephen. *The Existence and Attributes of God.* 1682. Reprint. Grand Rapids: Baker, 1979.

2

Two Denials
of the Biblical Doctrine

Not all theologians are content with the doctrine that God foreknows the future free acts of individuals. Hence two sorts of denial of this doctrine have been issued: (1) denial that God has foreknowledge of such events, and (2) denial that there are any truly free acts. The first affirms that some acts are free but denies that God foreknows them, while the second affirms that God completely foreknows the future but denies that there are any free acts for God to foreknow. Let us examine each of these views in turn.

Denial of Divine Foreknowledge

According to the first denial, the Bible does not teach that God has complete knowledge of the future. He can only make intelligent conjectures about what free persons are going to do. In fact, God is ignorant of vast stretches of forthcoming history, since even a single significant human choice could turn history in a different direction, and subsequent events would, as time goes on, be increasingly different from his expectations. At best God can be said to have a good idea of what will happen only in the very near future.

Now such a view seems so obviously unbiblical that the reader might well be surprised that anyone could believe that it represents the biblical teaching. Those who hold to it, however, typically point to passages in the Scripture in which God is depicted as ignorant of some fact. For example, when he visited Abraham, God said, "Because the outcry against Sodom and Gomorrah is great and their sin is very grave, I will go down to see whether they have done altogether according to the outcry which has come to me; and if not, I will know" (Gen. 18:20–21). In other cases, God seems unsure of how people will react to his prophetic messages. For example, God commands Jeremiah to prophesy to the cities of Judah and adds, "It may be they will listen, and every one turn from his evil way, that I may repent of the evil which I intend to do to them because of their evil doings" (Jer. 26:3). Later God says to his prophet, "It may be that the house of Judah will hear all the evil which I intend to do to them, so that every one may turn from his evil way, and that I may forgive their iniquity and their sin" (Jer. 36:3). Similarly, in commanding Ezekiel to perform a prophetic sign, God says, "Perhaps they will understand, though they are a rebellious house" (Ezek. 12:3). God here seems as ignorant about the future free reactions of his people as are the prophets themselves.

The problem with trying to base a doctrine of God's knowledge on such passages, however, is that some of them are clearly anthropomorphic in character, that is, God is described in human terms which are not intended to be taken literally. Thus, references in Scripture to God's eyes, hands, and nostrils, or to his seeing, hearing, crushing, turning, and so forth, are *metaphors*, since God does not possess literal bodily parts. In the same way, the passages which portray God as ignorant or inquiring are probably anthropomorphic metaphors. This should be obvious in the case of the Lord's visit to Abraham, for the context indicates that God appeared to him in the guise of three men. The Lord's speaking of "go[ing] down to see" what is happening is a clear anthropomorphism, since God himself has no body. In any case, taking these verses literally denies to God not foreknowledge, but knowledge of what has been and is presently going on. But certainly God has such knowledge; in fact, in the very same chapter God displays clairvoyant knowledge of the present (Gen. 18:12–15).

As for the prophecies in which God states that perhaps the people will repent, this comment does not seem to be an expression of ignorance on God's part, but rather an assurance to the listeners that it is not too late for them to change and avert disaster. As Jeremiah says, "Now therefore amend your ways and your doings, and obey the voice of the LORD your God, and the LORD will repent of the evil which he has pronounced against you" (Jer. 26:13). There is no implication that God did not know how the people would react. On the contrary, God seemed to know all too well in Ezekiel's case that the people would not respond, but God insisted that his prophet faithfully proclaim the message whether the people listened or not (Ezek. 2:5, 7; 33:31–33). Similarly, in the prophecy of Isaiah it is evident that God foreknew all along that Israel would not respond: "For I knew that you would deal very treacherously, and that from birth you were called a rebel" (Isa. 48:8).

Those who deny divine foreknowledge also appeal to passages in which God predicts that something will happen, but then repents, so that the predicted event does not come to pass (Amos 7:1–6; Jon. 3; Isa. 38:1–5). Obviously, since what God predicted did not in the end happen, the predictions were not foreknowledge of the future. Our problem here is how to explain how it is that while the authors of these passages were aware that God knew the future and could not lie (Num. 23:19; 1 Sam. 15:29), yet they represent him as relenting on impending judgments which he had commanded his prophets to proclaim.

The most plausible interpretation of such passages is that the prophecies contained the implicit condition "all things remaining the same." These prophecies were not simple glimpses of the future, but pictures of what was going to happen *unless. . . .* Prophecies with such conditions are not unusual in the Old Testament. One thinks of Abraham's intercession for Sodom and Gomorrah (Gen. 18:16–32), Abraham and Isaac at Moriah (Gen. 22:1–14), or David's fasting for his dying son (2 Sam. 12:14–23). David later recalled the reasoning behind his fasting even though the boy's death was prophesied: "While the child was still alive, I fasted and wept; for I said, 'Who knows whether the LORD will be gracious to me, that the child may live?'" (2 Sam. 12:22; cf. Jon. 3:9).

Thus the reaction of Hezekiah, Amos, and the people of Nineveh was entirely appropriate: one simply did not know whether the prophecy contained conditions that made it possible to avert disaster. Sometimes such conditions might be explicit, as they were in Jeremiah's prophecy to King Zedekiah:

> Thus says the LORD, the God of hosts, the God of Israel, If you will surrender to the princes of the king of Babylon, then your life shall be spared, and this city shall not be burned with fire, and you and your house shall live. But if you do not surrender . . . , then this city shall be given into the hand of the Chaldeans, and they shall burn it with fire, and you shall not escape from their hand. [Jer. 38:17–18]

This passage illustrates human freedom within God's sovereign control, but in no way implies that God did not foreknow the choice which Zedekiah would make. Rather, opportunity was being left for the king to avert impending disaster. As the Lord later declared through the prophet Ezekiel, "Though I say to the wicked, 'You shall surely die,' yet if he turns from his sin and does what is lawful and right, . . . he shall surely live, he shall not die" (Ezek. 33:14–15).

If our argument is correct, then certain prophecies do not represent bits of foreknowledge, but rather are forecasts or forewarnings of what is going to happen if all things remain as they are. But not all of the prophecies in the Old and New Testaments are like this. Prophecies of events which could not have been inferred from present causes and which were brought about not by God but by human beings cannot be interpreted as forewarnings, but must be considered to express genuine foreknowledge on God's part. Moreover, even if the problematic passages considered thus far are not anthropomorphisms or conditional forewarnings, they still do not serve to overturn the clear teaching of Scripture elsewhere, which we examined in chapter 1, that God does foreknow the future free acts of individuals. One still could not deny that the Scriptures in their most exalted and thoughtful vision of God portray him as completely omniscient, knowing even future free acts.

How do the detractors of foreknowledge explain these passages? Typically, they attempt to dismiss each example of divine foreknowledge in Scripture as being one of the following:

1. a declaration by God of what he himself intends to bring about
2. an inference of what is going to happen based on present causes

3. a conditional prediction of what will happen *if* something else happens

Such an account seems inadequate, however. As far as (3) is concerned, conditional predictions, if they do not reduce to (1) or (2), must be expressions of divine middle knowledge (to be discussed in chapter 12), which is even more remarkable than divine foreknowledge and, indeed, may provide the basis for divine foreknowledge. Hence, to try to explain away divine foreknowledge by means of (3) is counterproductive.

As for (2), while it might be claimed, say, that Jesus predicted Judas's betrayal or Peter's denial solely on the basis of their character and the surrounding circumstances, there can be no question that the Gospel writers themselves did not so understand such predictions. As I argued earlier (p. 36), to try to explain biblical prophecies as mere inferences from present states of affairs denudes them of any theological significance. The writers of Scripture clearly saw prophecy not as God's reasoned conjecture of what will happen, but as a manifestation of his infinite knowledge, encompassing even things yet to come.

As for (1), many prophecies in Scripture are clearly based on God's irrevocable intention to bring about certain future events on his own. As God affirms in the Book of Isaiah,

> The former things I declared of old,
>   they went forth from my mouth and I made them known;
>   then suddenly I did them and they came to pass.
>
> [Isa. 48:3]

In such cases, prophecy serves to manifest not so much God's omniscience as his omnipotence, his ability to bring about whatever he intends. But the problem with (1) is that it simply cannot be stretched to cover all the cases. Remember, the denial now under discussion holds that many human actions are genuinely free. Divine foreknowledge of such actions cannot be accounted for by (1), since it negates human freedom. Explanation (1) is useful only in accounting for God's knowledge of events which he himself will bring about. But the Scripture provides many examples of divine foreknowledge of events which God does not directly cause, events which are the result of free human choices. And even in prophecies concerning God's own actions, foreknowledge of free human acts is sometimes presupposed. For example, when God speaks of using Cyrus to subdue the nations (Isa. 44:28–45:1), God's intention presupposes his foreknowledge that such a person shall in fact come to exist at the proper time and place and be in a position to serve as God's instrument. To respond that God brings about all these details as well would be to deny the very human freedom which the view we are discussing wants to affirm.

Finally, none of the three explanations comes to grips with the Scriptures' doctrinal teaching concerning God's foreknowledge. These explanations try to account only for examples of prophecy in the Bible and say nothing about the passages which explicitly teach that God foreknows the future.

In summary, the first denial of the biblical doctrine of divine foreknowledge is just not very plausible. Passages attributing ignorance to God are clearly anthropomorphic. Passages speaking of God's repenting, so that what he has predicted will happen does not in fact come to pass, have to do only with forewarnings which include the implicit condition "all things remaining the same." In any case, such passages do not negate the fact that in its most profound concept of God Scripture affirms divine foreknowledge of future free acts. Attempts to explain away all the prophecies of Scripture without recourse to foreknowledge seem futile and do not in any event address the portions of Scripture which explicitly teach divine omniscience. Hence I conclude that, given that certain human actions are freely chosen, divine foreknowledge of such actions cannot be biblically denied.

Denial of Human Freedom

According to the second denial of the doctrine that God foreknows future free acts, God does foreknow all future events, including human choices and actions, but only because none of them are genuinely free. Jewish religion had a strong sense of God's sovereignty, and there is a stream of texts running through Scripture which imply that literally everything which happens is ordained by God to happen. Hence it might be said that he foreknows the future because he foreordains everything that will occur. While too numerous for us to list, the texts which have led to this view have been collected by D. A. Carson under four main headings: (1) God is the Creator, Ruler, and Possessor of all things; (2) God is the ultimate personal cause of all that happens; (3) God elects his people; and (4) God is the un-acknowledged source of good fortune or success.[1] Carson concludes:

> With such sweeping sovereignty at his disposal, Yahweh's predic-tions concerning what will take place in the future, and his con-trol over that future, cannot always be decisively distinguished (cf. Gen. 15:13–16; 25:22f.; 41:16, 25, 32; Josh. 6:26 and I Kgs. 16:34; Isa. 46:8–10; 48:5f.). What he decrees must come to pass.[2]

Looking closely at the texts cited by Carson, we find that his conclusion seems overdrawn. In the prediction to Abraham there is no suggestion that God would cause Israel to be in bondage four hundred years, but only that he would bring her out. Similarly, in Genesis 25 there is no suggestion of foreor-dination in connection with Esau and Jacob (though, it must be admitted, Paul in Rom. 9:10–13 seems to make such an inter-pretation). Joshua 6:26 and 1 Kings 16:34 do not concern fore-knowledge at all, but a curse and its later fulfilment. On the other hand, Genesis 41:25 does seem to suggest that what God had given to Joseph was not so much foreknowledge as a revela-tion of what God intended to do. Similarly, Isaiah's predictions seem to disclose what God intended to do in judgment on Israel. In this case, God's foreknowledge would seem to be based on his irrevocable intention to do something and his knowledge that he can bring about whatever he intends.

This presents only half the picture, however. For the convic-tion that human beings are free moral agents also permeates the Hebrew way of thinking; there is no hint of a fatalism which reduces humans to mere puppets. Throughout the Scriptures

---

1. D. A. Carson, *Divine Sovereignty and Human Responsibility: Biblical Perspectives in Tension,* New Foundations Theological Library (Atlanta: John Knox, 1981), pp. 24–35.

2. Ibid., p. 26.

are texts which seem to presuppose genuine human freedom before God. Carson lists them under nine heads: (1) people face a multitude of divine exhortations and commands; (2) people are said to obey, believe, and choose God; (3) people sin and rebel against God; (4) their sins are judged by God; (5) people are tested by God; (6) people receive divine rewards; (7) the elect are responsible to respond to God's initiative; (8) prayers are not mere showpieces scripted by God; and (9) God literally pleads with sinners to repent and be saved.[3] These texts suggest a great measure of human freedom in our intercourse with God.

Perhaps one of the most striking indications of this freedom is the passages which speak of God's repenting (e.g., Gen. 6:6; 1 Sam. 15:11, 35). It is not clear to what extent the proponents of the view that foreknowledge is invariably the consequence of foreordination can plausibly explain away these texts as pure anthropomorphisms. Such thinkers might interpret these verses as meaning that when individuals continue in sin, they will be judged, but God will forgive them if they repent. The change, then, is on the individual's part, not God's.[4] But even this minimal understanding underscores that God's sovereignty is not a blind force acting irrespective of human actions, but is contingent in certain cases upon human decisions.

Moreover, it does not seem that all predictions or instances of foreknowledge in the Scriptures can be explained in terms of foreordination. For there are instances of foreknowledge of events which God does not bring about. For example, we have seen that God foreknows our thoughts; any attempt to reduce such foreknowledge to foreordination would seem to lead to the sort of determinism which Jewish thought rejects. Carson counters that there are many cases in the Old Testament where human thoughts and decisions *are* attributed directly to God's determining (2 Sam. 24:1; Isa. 19:13–14; 37:7; Prov. 21:1; Ezra

---

3. Ibid., pp. 18–22.

4. See H. Van Dyke Parunak, "A Semantic Survey of *NHM*," *Biblica* 56 (1975): 512–32. According to Parunak, in passages such as Gen. 6:6 and 1 Sam. 15:11, 35, "repent" means "to suffer emotional pain." In other contexts, it may mean "to retract blessing or judgment" on the basis of a change in human conduct which has rendered the promised blessing or threatened judgment inappropriate.

1:1; 7:6, 27–28; Neh. 2:11–12).[5] These references, however, are not very convincing and do not even approach a universal determinism.

Furthermore, we have seen numerous instances of God's foreknowledge of future sinful acts—can these acts be ascribed to God's foreordination? Carson claims that the Old Testament writers do not shy away from making God himself in some mysterious way the cause of many evils (1 Kings 22:19–22; 2 Sam. 24:1; Gen. 50:20; Judg. 9:23; 1 Sam. 16:14; Job 1:6–12; Amos 3:6).[6] But he admits that most of these references concern God's judgment on sin; in the remaining cases of Joseph and Job it seems plausible that God permits some evil in order to bring about a greater good. Moreover, Carson admits that the Scriptures do sometimes distinguish between what God does (good) and what humans do (evil) (Ezek. 11:16–21; Ps. 78; Eccles. 7:29). Carson also concedes that there is in the Scriptures a sort of asymmetry in the way in which our deeds are ascribed ultimately to God: "The manner in which God stands behind evil and the manner in which he stands behind good are not precisely identical; for he is to be praised for the good, but not blamed for the evil."[7] But if God foreordains and brings about evil thoughts and deeds, it seems impossible to give an adequate account of this biblical asymmetry. Even the most radical theologian who believes that God foreordains every action must allow human beings a certain freedom of thought and intention if God is not to be regarded as the author of sin. How to explain Adam's fall without implicating God must be particularly nettlesome for such a theologian. It would seem more plausible to maintain that God sovereignly permits us freedom to sin against him. The difference between his willing good and his permitting evil seems to provide a plausible basis for the biblical asymmetry that Carson notes. All good ultimately comes from God, whereas evil derives from creaturely misuse of freedom. Whatever explanation of evil one adopts, the central point here is that God's foreknowledge of evil deeds (say, Judas's betrayal or

---

5. Carson, *Divine Sovereignty*, p. 27.
6. Ibid., p. 29.
7. Ibid., p. 212.

Peter's denial) cannot be accounted for on the basis that God has predestined everything that comes to pass.

Therefore, even if we allow that many of the biblical prophecies are based on foreordination, it nevertheless seems clear that God's foreknowledge of many other future events cannot be so explained. For the Bible teaches that humans have genuine freedom, and that in many cases what God does depends on how they respond to his initiatives. His foreknowledge of the future cannot be based on foreordination alone, for he foreknows our thoughts and intentions and even our sinful acts. Since God is not responsible for these human activities, it follows that he does not bring them about. They are therefore truly free acts, or contingents, and God's foreknowledge of them is thus foreknowledge of future free actions.

We have seen that the biblical view of God's omniscience includes knowledge of all past, present, and future states of affairs. In particular, he knows future free acts, a knowledge essential to the biblical view of history. Any denial, therefore, that God knows future free acts is subbiblical and ought to be rejected by the Christian theologian and philosopher of religion.

Suggested Further Reading

Carson, D. A. *Divine Sovereignty and Human Responsibility: Biblical Perspectives in Tension.* New Foundations Theological Library. Atlanta: John Knox, 1981.

Basinger, David, and Randall Basinger, eds. *Predestination and Free Will.* Downers Grove, Ill.: Inter-Varsity, 1986.

PART 2

The Compatibility of Divine Foreknowledge and Human Freedom

3

The Argument
for Theological Fatalism

We have seen in part 1 that the Bible affirms God's foreknowledge of future free acts of human beings. But a number of modern philosophers have argued that such a doctrine is incoherent. Divine foreknowledge and human freedom, they say, are mutually exclusive; if one is affirmed, the other must be denied.

In order to understand the reasoning that undergirds this objection to the biblical view of God and man, let us examine the argument put forward by Nelson Pike, one of the most influential contemporary proponents of theological fatalism. In 1965, while professor of philosophy at Cornell University, Pike published an article entitled "Divine Omniscience and Voluntary Action," in which he argued that if an omniscient God exists, then no human action is free.[1] Pike confessed that his argument had a "sharp, counterintuitive ring," but still he believed that it proved that divine foreknowledge and human freedom are incompatible.

---

1. Nelson Pike, "Divine Omniscience and Voluntary Action," *Philosophical Review* 74 (1965): 27–46; see also the revised version in Nelson Pike, *God and Timelessness*, Studies in Ethics and the Philosophy of Religion (London: Routledge & Kegan Paul; New York: Schocken, 1970), chap. 4. Technically, Pike is not a theological fatalist, for he attempts to escape fatalism by arguing that God could be timeless and thus would not literally foreknow anything. Unfortunately, as we shall see (pp. 63–65), this escape route is unavailing. Moreover, since Pike later denies that God is timeless, this escape route is not in any case open to him.

Pike invites us to consider some hypothetical individual named Jones, who on Saturday afternoon mows his lawn. Since God is omniscient, he knew eighty years ago that Jones would mow his lawn on Saturday afternoon. And since God cannot be mistaken, when Saturday afternoon arrives, Jones is not able to refrain from mowing his lawn. God's belief that Jones would mow his lawn is "tucked away" in the past and cannot be changed, so that Jones cannot affect it in any way. Since God's beliefs are infallible, Jones does not have it within his power to do anything other than what God believes he will do.

Pike formulates his argument in several steps:

1. God's being omniscient necessarily implies that if Jones mows his lawn on Saturday afternoon, then God believed at an earlier time that Jones would mow his lawn on Saturday afternoon.
2. Necessarily, all of God's beliefs are true.
3. No one has the power to make a contradiction true.
4. No one has the power to erase someone's past beliefs, that is, to bring it about that something believed in the past by someone was not believed in the past by that person.
5. No one has the power to erase someone's existence in the past, that is, to bring it about that someone who existed in the past did not exist in the past.
6. So if God believed that Jones would mow his lawn on Saturday afternoon, Jones can refrain from mowing his lawn only if one of the following alternatives is true:
   i. Jones has the power to make God's belief false;
   ii. Jones has the power to erase God's past belief; or
   iii. Jones has the power to erase God's past existence.
7. But alternative (i) is impossible. (This follows from steps 2 and 3.)
8. And alternative (ii) is impossible. (This follows from step 4.)
9. And alternative (iii) is impossible. (This follows from step 5.)
10. Therefore, if God believes that Jones will mow his lawn on Saturday afternoon, Jones does not have the power to

refrain from mowing his lawn on Saturday afternoon; that is to say, Jones is not free.

By extension, no person is free with regard to any of his or her actions.

As for the respective steps of this argument, (1) and (2) are simply an explication of what it means to be omniscient and are therefore true. Steps (3), (4), and (5) are expressions of ways in which our power is limited. Pike believes that each of these steps is obviously true according to common sense. Step (6) states in effect that there are only three alternatives if Jones is to be free. If one could think up some fourth alternative, one could escape Pike's argument, but Pike apparently thinks that there are only these three. Steps (7), (8), and (9) simply eliminate each respective alternative by appealing to the earlier limitations on power. After the elimination of each of the three alternatives, step (10) states the conclusion that if God has foreknowledge, then Jones is not free.

It is interesting to note that Pike does not think that human foreknowledge of the future implies fatalism. He invites us to consider the case of Smith, an intimate friend of Jones. Smith knows that Jones normally mows his lawn Saturday afternoons, and he knows that Jones fully intends to do the same this Saturday. Therefore, we may say that Smith foreknows that Jones will mow his lawn Saturday afternoon. But if this is the case, then when Saturday afternoon arrives, is not Jones fated to mow his lawn, just as he allegedly is when God foreknows his action? No, answers Pike, because in this case Jones does have the power to falsify Smith's belief. Jones can refrain from mowing his lawn, and if he does, then Smith was simply mistaken. But Jones cannot falsify God's belief, since God is infallible and cannot be mistaken. So while divine foreknowledge implies fatalism, human foreknowledge does not.

But wait a minute! If Smith really *knows* that Jones will mow his lawn this Saturday, then he cannot be mistaken; otherwise he would only *believe* it. So if Jones refrains, then Smith did not foreknow that Jones would mow the lawn; he just mistakenly believed it. But if we suppose that Smith really does know that Jones will mow his lawn on Saturday, then Jones must mow his lawn on Saturday, for if he can refrain, then he has the power to bring it about that Smith's true belief is also false, which is self-contradictory.

Pike, however, has a subtle response to this objection. From the fact that Smith foreknows Jones's action, it follows only that Jones *will* in fact mow his lawn, not that he *must* mow his lawn. He will not refrain from mowing the lawn, but he still has the power to refrain. If he *were* to refrain, then Smith's belief (which is in fact true) *would have been* false. While Jones does not have the power to bring it about that Smith's true belief was also false, he does have the power to bring it about that Smith's belief, while in fact true, *would have been* false. Thus, human foreknowledge does not imply fatalism.

This solution, Pike maintains, does not work in the case of divine foreknowledge. For one cannot say that God's belief, while in fact true, could have been false. For God's beliefs are infallibly true; it is impossible that he make a mistake. Hence it makes no sense to say that if Jones were to refrain, God's belief would have been false. For if God foreknows Jones's action, Jones does not have the power to refrain; otherwise he would have the power to bring it about that God's belief, which is in fact true, would have been false, which does not make sense. Pike admits that if it can be shown that human foreknowledge, no less than divine foreknowledge, implies fatalism, then his argument ought to be rejected. But he believes that he has shown the essential difference between the two, namely, human foreknowledge is not infallible, but God's is.

Pike's reasoning is typical of the arguments for theological fatalism. It is important that the reader, before proceeding further, understand Pike's argument. If it is correct, then God's foreknowledge of the future cannot be reconciled with human freedom.

Suggested Further Reading

Pike, Nelson. *God and Timelessness.* Studies in Ethics and the Philosophy of Religion. London: Routledge & Kegan Paul; New York: Schocken, 1970. Chapter 4.

Prior, Arthur N. "The Formalities of Omniscience." In Arthur N. Prior, *Papers on Time and Tense,* pp. 26–44. Oxford: Clarendon, 1968.

4

Three Unsuccessful Attempts
to Escape Fatalism

Most thinkers who have presented the argument for theological fatalism have also attempted to escape it, suggesting ways in which one could hold to both divine omniscience and human freedom. In this chapter we shall look at three proposed escape routes to see if they afford any way out of the dilemma. As this chapter is somewhat technical and not essential to our argument, the more casual reader may prefer to skip it and go directly to chapter 5.

Proposal 1: *"Future-Tense Statements Are Neither True Nor False"*

The escape route most commonly suggested by would-be fatalists is that future-tense statements about free acts, such as "a woman will be elected president in 1992," are neither true nor false. An omniscient being would not know the truth of such statements, since there is no truth to know. Therefore, even if God lacks foreknowledge, he is still omniscient, for he knows all the truth there is to know.

The view that future-tense statements are neither true nor false cannot, however, be plausibly maintained. Here several points need to be made:

1. *There is no good reason to deny that future-tense statements are either true or false.* Why should we accept the view that future-tense statements about free acts, statements which

55

we use all the time in ordinary conversation, are in fact neither true nor false? What proof is there that such statements are neither true nor false?

About the only answer of any substance ever given to this question goes something like this: Future events, unlike present events, do not exist. That is to say, the future is not "out there," waiting somewhere in the distance for us to arrive. The 1992 presidential election, for instance, does not in any sense exist. To suppose that it does is to spatialize time, that is, to think of time as a line with future events stretched out in one direction and past events stretched out in the other. But time is not like a line that is stretched out; time has a front edge, so to speak, namely, the present moment, and events which are future to this moment are entirely nonexistent. Now, this attempt to answer fatalism continues, a statement is true if and only if it corresponds to what exists, and false if and only if it does not correspond to what exists. Since the future does not exist, there is nothing for future-tense statements to correspond with or to fail to correspond with. Hence, future-tense statements cannot be true or false.

Now since I am inclined to accept the view of time which this proposed answer to fatalism adopts, the issue is whether, given such a view, the definition of truth as correspondence requires us to deny that future-tense statements are either true or false. Those who think that it does seem to misunderstand the concept of truth as correspondence, which holds merely that a statement is true if and only if what it states to be the case really is the case. For example, the statement "it is snowing" is true if and only if it is snowing. Although this might seem too obvious to be worth stating, it is sometimes misunderstood. Truth as correspondence does *not* mean that the things or events which a true statement is about must exist. Indeed, it is only in the case of true present-tense statements that the things or events referred to must exist. For example, "President Reagan is signing the tax-reform bill" is true if and only if Reagan is now signing the tax-reform bill—the statement is true at the moment the event happens. But with true statements in other tenses, the things or events described need not exist. For example, "Reagan won the 1980 presidential election" is true if and only if Reagan won the 1980 presidential election. For this statement to be true, the election cannot be happening now; the tense of the statement requires that the event described happened before the statement became true. Long after the election is over, indeed, long after Reagan has ceased to exist, this past-tense statement will still be true. For the statement to be true it is not required that what it describes exist, but only that it *have* existed. All that is necessary is that in 1980 the present-tense statement "Reagan wins the presidential election" was true. Similarly, the future-tense statement "a woman will win the 1992 presidential election" is true if and only if a woman will win the 1992 presidential election. For the statement to be true it is not required that the election somehow exist, but that it *will* exist. In order for this future-tense statement to be true, all that is required is that when the moment described arrives, the present-tense version of the statement will be true; that is, that "a woman wins the presidential election" will be true in 1992. That the concept of truth as correspondence requires that the things or events described by the statement must exist at the time the statement is true is a complete misunderstanding.

To say that a future-tense statement is now true is not, of course, to say that we may now know whether it is true or to say that things are now so determined that it is true. It is only to say that when the time arrives, things will turn out as the statement predicts. Nicholas Rescher and Alasdair Urquhart in their text *Temporal Logic* conclude,

> The issue of truth or falsity hinges entirely upon *how matters turn out at the time at issue,* so that the allocation of a truth status to future contingents is perfectly innocuous, because it prejudges nothing. No suggestion is intended that the truth status a future contingent proposition certainly *has* at times prior to the time of reference can be *specified* at these earlier times without any reference to "how matters turn out."[1]

A future-tense statement is true if matters turn out as the statement predicts, and false if matters fail to turn out as the statement predicts—this is all that the notion of truth as

---

1. Nicholas Rescher and Alasdair Urquhart, *Temporal Logic,* Library of Exact Philosophy (New York: Springer-Verlag, 1971), p. 211.

correspondence requires. Hence there is no good reason to deny that future-tense statements are either true or false.

2. *There are good reasons to maintain that future-tense statements are either true or false.* Not only is there no good reason to deny the truth or falsity of future-tense statements, but there are, on the contrary, good reasons to affirm that they are either true or false.

 a. The same facts that make present- and past-tense statements true or false also make future-tense statements true or false. Rescher explains,

> Difficulties about divine foreknowledge quite apart, it is difficult to justify granting to
>
> 1. "It will rain tomorrow" (asserted on April 12)
>
> a truth status different from that of
>
> 2. "It did rain yesterday" (asserted on April 14)
>
> because both make (from temporally distinct perspectives) *precisely the same claim about the facts,* viz., rain on April 13.[2]

Think about it for a moment. If "it is raining today" is now true, how could "it will rain tomorrow" not have been true yesterday? The same facts make a future-tense statement asserted earlier, a present-tense statement asserted simultaneously, and a past-tense statement asserted later all true.

 b. If future-tense statements are not true, then neither are past-tense statements. If future-tense statements cannot be true because the realities they describe do not yet exist, then by the same token past-tense statements cannot be true because the realities they describe no longer exist. But to maintain that past-tense statements cannot be true would be ridiculous. If, then, we allow past-tense statements to be true, future-tense statements should also be allowed to be true. As Charles Bayliss explained in an important article published in the journal *Philosophy of Science:*

---

2. Nicholas Rescher, *Many-Valued Logic* (New York: McGraw-Hill, 1969), pp. 2–3.

> For the truth of propositions to the effect that certain events did occur in the past it is necessary only that the occurrence of these events was at the time specified a fact, and, similarly, for the truth of propositions to the effect that certain events will occur at a given time in the future it is necessary only that the occurrence of these events at that time will be a fact.[3]

Since the two cases are parallel, one must either deny the truth or falsity of both past- and future-tense statements or affirm the truth or falsity of both.

c. Tenseless statements are always true or false. It is possible to eliminate the tense of the verb in a statement by specifying the time at which the statement is supposed to be true. For example, the statement "the Allies invaded Normandy" can be made tenseless by specifying the time: "on June 6, 1944, the Allies *invade* Normandy," the italics indicating the verb is tenseless. Now as Thomas Talbott points out, even though tensed statements cannot be put into a tenseless form without some loss of meaning, still, if the tensed version is true, then so is the tenseless version.[4] Thus, correlated with any true past- or present-tense statement is a true tenseless version of that statement. Furthermore, as Talbott points out, a tenseless statement, if it is true at all, is *always* true. This is precisely because the statement is tenseless. If "on June 6, 1944, the Allies *invade* Normandy" is *ever* true, then it is *always* true. Therefore, this statement is true prior to June 6, 1944. But in that case, it is true prior to June 6, 1944, that the Allies on that date will invade Normandy, which is the same as saying that the future-tense version of the tenseless statement is true. Moreover, since God is omniscient, he must always know the truth of the tenseless statement, a fact which entails that he foreknows the future.

3. *The denial of the truth or falsity of future-tense statements has absurd consequences.* For example, if future-tense statements are neither true nor false, the statement "George Bush either will or will not win the presidential election in 1992" would not be true. For this statement is a compound

---

3. Charles A. Bayliss, "Are Some Propositions Neither True Nor False?" *Philosophy of Science* 3 (1936): 162.

4. Thomas Bradley Talbott, "Fatalism and the Timelessness of Truth" (Ph.D. diss., University of California at Santa Barbara, 1974), pp. 153–54.

sentence made up of two simple future-tense sentences—"Bush will win the presidential election in 1992" and "Bush will not win the presidential election in 1992." And if neither of these individual statements is true or false, the compound statement combining them is also neither true nor false. But how can this be? Either Bush will win or he will not—there is no other alternative. But the view that future-tense statements are neither true nor false would require us to say that this compound statement is neither true nor false, which seems absurd.

Worse still, we could not say that a statement like "Bush both will and will not win the presidential election in 1992" is false. For this is a compound statement consisting of two simple future-tense statements, neither of which is supposed to be true or false. Therefore, the compound statement cannot be true or false either. But surely this statement is false, for it is a self-contradiction: Bush cannot both win and not win the election!

We must conclude that with no good reason in favor of it, persuasive reasons against it, and absurd consequences following from it, the view that future-tense statements about free decisions are neither true nor false is untenable and provides no escape from fatalism. Moreover, the view that God's omniscience does not encompass foreknowledge is also thereby seen to be untenable, since he must know the truth of all true future-tense statements.

Proposal 2: *"All Future-Tense Statements Are False"*

The Oxford logician Arthur N. Prior proposed a different escape from fatalism: he held that all future-tense statements about free actions are false.[5] Now at face value this suggestion seems very queer. For if it is false that "Bush will win the 1992 presidential election," then surely it is true that "Bush will not win the 1992 presidential election." For to say a statement is false is tantamount to saying that the negation of that statement

---

5. Arthur N. Prior, "The Formalities of Omniscience," in Arthur N. Prior, *Papers on Time and Tense* (Oxford: Clarendon, 1968), pp. 38–40; see also "Identifiable Individuals," pp. 66–77.

is true. Hence, if it is false that Bush will win, it is true that he will not win. But Prior's proposal requires us to say that both of these statements are false.

Prior tries to get around the problem by reinterpreting what the negation of a future-tense statement is. He rejects, for example, the form:

Affirmation: Bush will win the election.

Negation: Bush will not win the election.

in favor of

Affirmation: Bush will win the election.

Negation: It is not the case that Bush will win the election.

That is to say, when we form the negation of a future-tense statement, we should do so by prefacing the affirmation with "it is not the case that. . . ." In this way, the negation of a future-tense statement is always true, since all future-tense statements are false. If the future-tense statement is itself negative, for example, "Bush will not win the election," the negation is still true, namely, "it is not the case that Bush will not win the election." Hence, it is not now the case that Bush will win, and it is not now the case that he will not win. Neither of these is now the case because there is a "gap in the facts," for the election has not yet occurred.

Now Prior was a great logician, but it seems clear that he made a mistake in his reinterpretation of what the negation of a future-tense statement is. The use of expressions like "it is the case," "it was the case," and "it will be the case," is a device of philosophers to eliminate the tense of the verb in a sentence. For example, we can render "Reagan won the 1980 election" as "it was the case that Reagan wins the 1980 election." The tense of the verb is transferred to the clause "it was the case." With regard to our previous example, the affirmation and negation should then be:

Affirmation: It will be the case that Bush wins the election.

Negation: It will not be the case that Bush wins the election.

Here there is no gap in the facts, for the statements assert merely that at some future time Bush's election or loss will be the case.

Prior would say that the negation is still in an incorrect form. Rather it should be:

Affirmation: It will be the case that Bush wins the election.

Negation: It is not the case that it will be the case that Bush wins the election.

But does such a reinterpretation make any difference at all? To say that it is not the case that Bush's election will be the case seems to be the same as saying that Bush's election will not be the case. Regardless, what reason is there for preferring Prior's reinterpretation, with all its ambiguity, to the normal understanding of negation?

Prior's answer is that statements about individuals who do not yet exist cannot be true, because nobody exists for the statements to be about. Inasmuch as the statement "William Willis will be president in 2050" does not refer to someone who exists, it cannot be true. There is no such person as William Willis. Therefore, no statement about him can be true.

We can respond to Prior in either of two ways: (1) Before creating the world, God knew all the logically possible worlds he could create, populated by all the logically possible individuals he could create. William Willis is a member of some of those possible worlds, and in some of them he is president in 2050. Since God knows which world he has created, he knows whether or not the actual world is a world in which Willis will be president. Hence, individuals who do not yet exist can be identified on the basis of God's knowing all logically possible worlds, all logically possible individuals, and the world and individuals he has chosen to actually create.

(2) We can, like Prior, conceive of the present as branching off into various directions, each representing a different possible future course of events. By providing complete and accurate

descriptions in terms of genealogy, place, time, and so forth, we can pick out possible individuals on particular branches. Of course, we do not know which branch represents the actual future, but that does not stop us from referring to nonexistent individuals and making statements about them. Hence, a statement about William Willis, if we make clear whose descendant he is supposed to be, can be true and will be true if the branch we have in mind should turn out to be the actual future.

Another shortcoming of Prior's view is that even if it were acceptable, it would still fail to escape fatalism. For as individuals come to be born and exist, future-tense statements about them would become true or false. Hence his view would lead to a sort of "creeping fatalism," as individuals come to exist and statements about them become true.

Finally, Prior's view leads to an absurd consequence. For in his view, if one says, "Bush will win the presidential election in 1992," and in 1992 Bush does win, we still have to say that the future-tense statement was false. But this seems absurd, for what else does it mean for a future-tense statement to be true than for things to turn out as the statement says they will? Prior himself confesses that his view has this "perverse" consequence and sees no way to avoid it.

With no reason to commend it, an absurd consequence following from it, and creeping fatalism implied by it, Prior's view does not provide a plausible answer to fatalism.

Proposal 3: *"Truth and God Are Timeless"*

Other philosophers have sought to elude fatalism by maintaining that all statements are timelessly true or false and therefore are not literally true *in advance of* the events they predict. This view requires that all tensed statements be put into tenseless versions by specifying the date, as we did before, and by eliminating any references which reflect the speaker's point of view. For example, the sentence "tomorrow I shall leave here and travel to Paris" becomes the tenseless statement "on November 21, 1985, William Craig *leaves* Amsterdam and *travels* to Paris." Such a statement is timelessly true. Because they are not true *before* the events, nothing is fated by such statements.

In a similar way, certain theologians have held that God is timeless and has timeless knowledge of all events, whether these events are to us past, present, or future. Therefore, he does not literally *fore*know anything, and so nothing can be fated by his knowledge.

The view that all tensed sentences can be translated into tenseless statements without loss of meaning has, however, come under broad attack. For example, "today is March 15, 1977," certainly says more than "March 15, 1977, is March 15, 1977." But that point aside, it is not clear that tenseless statements are in fact timelessly true. Most of the advocates of tenseless statements take them to be true at *all* times rather than timelessly true. William Kneale, coauthor of the standard text *Development of Logic,* associates timelessness of truth only with mathematical, metaphysical, and necessary scientific truths.[6] His coauthor, Martha Kneale, goes even further:

> All that is meant by calling mathematical truths "timeless" is that there is no point in asking when two and two are four in the way that there is point in asking when the daffodils are in bloom. But this does not mean that it is not the case that two and two are four today, that they were four yesterday and will be four tomorrow. These statements are not meaningless or untrue, but simply so obvious as to be pointless.[7]

But if tenseless statements are true at all times rather than timelessly true, they are true in advance of the events they report, so that fatalism is not avoided.

Now a few philosophers might insist that tenseless statements are indeed timelessly true. They would think it bizarre to say that the statement "diamonds are made of carbon" was true on Christmas Eve of 1912. Such oddness, however, does not amount to much of an argument, as Martha Kneale points out. In any case, such an insistence would still not stave off fatalism.

---

6. William Kneale, "Time and Eternity in Theology," *Proceedings of the Aristotelian Society* 61 (1960–61): 98.

7. Martha Kneale, "Eternity and Sempiternity," *Proceedings of the Aristotelian Society* 69 (1968–69): 228.

For even if truth itself is timeless, still it may be truly asserted in advance of some event that that event occurs at its future time. For example, it may be truly asserted in 1985 that "Bush *wins* the 1992 presidential election," even if this statement is itself timelessly true. But the ability to truly assert some timelessly true proposition about future events is all fatalists need to get their argument going.

In the same way, even if God is timeless, fatalism is not thereby avoided. As Paul Helm explains, the statement "God knows timelessly that some event *occurs* in my future" would still be true in advance of the event.[8] As long as this statement is true prior to the event, fatalism will follow. If one insists that this statement is also timelessly true, still it may be truly asserted in advance that "God *knows* timelessly that this event occurs in my future," which is once more all the fatalist needs. Thus, even holding that truth and God are timeless will not suffice to enable us to elude fatalism.

None of the three suggestions, then, provides a plausible escape from fatalism. All of these proposed escape routes try to deny the first premise of Pike's argument, that omniscience necessarily implies foreknowledge. The first two proposals deny God knowledge of events future to us; the third concedes that he has such knowledge, and in that sense it is superior to the first two, but it likewise cannot escape fatalism. Therefore, the fatalist's argument needs to be examined at other points. Perhaps the solutions proposed thus far have erred in granting too much weight to the rest of the fatalist's reasoning.

Suggested Further Reading

Bayliss, Charles A. "Are Some Propositions Neither True Nor False?" *Philosophy of Science* 3 (1936): 156–66.

Haack, Susan. *Deviant Logic: Some Philosophical Issues.* Cambridge: Cambridge University Press, 1974. See chap. 3.

---

8. Paul Helm, "Timelessness and Foreknowledge," *Mind* 84 (1975): 524–27.

5
Theological Fatalism Rejected

Wnat, then, can be said in response to Nelson Pike's argument for theological fatalism? Before specifically examining his argument, two general remarks ought to be made.

Preliminary Remarks

The Reducibility of Theological to Logical Fatalism

First, theological fatalism is simply a variation of logical fatalism. That is to say, the addition of God's foreknowledge to the argument does not add anything that is not implied by the simple fact that certain future-tense statements are true. On this basis one could argue just as effectively that if Jones will mow his lawn on Saturday afternoon, then it was true eighty years ago that Jones would mow his lawn on Saturday afternoon. That is a past fact that cannot be changed. Therefore, when Saturday arrives Jones does not have the power to do differently. If he had the power to refrain, he would bring it about that either (1) the statements "Jones will mow the lawn" and "Jones will not mow the lawn" were both true, or (2) the statement "Jones will mow the lawn" was false after having been true. But nobody has the power to make a contradiction true or to annul the truth of a statement which was true in the past. Therefore fatalism follows.

Thus I am disposed to agree with both Richard Taylor (a fatalist) and Susan Haack (a nonfatalist) that theological fatalism is just a dressed-up form of ancient Greek logical fatalism, which was based on the simple fact that certain future-tense statements are true. According to Taylor, an omniscient God can be incorporated into the argument to convey the reasoning more easily to the unphilosophical mind, but such an assumption contributes nothing to the cogency of the argument.[1] Haack calls the argument for theological fatalism "a needlessly (and confusingly) elaborated version" of Greek fatalism; the addition of an omniscient God to the argument constitutes a "gratuitous detour" around the real issue, which is the truth or falsity of future-tense statements.[2]

This insight is important, for it takes the onus off the Christian or Jew who on the basis of the biblical teaching holds to divine foreknowledge. The issue is much broader and must concern anyone who holds future-tense statements about free decisions to be either true or false. For if the fatalist's reasoning is correct, the mere truth of future-tense statements about future free acts implies that these acts happen necessarily.

The Unintelligibility of Fatalism

Second, fatalism is intuitively unintelligible, and therefore the argument in support of it must be fallacious. I am reminded in this connection of Zeno's paradoxes of motion. The ancient Greek philosopher Zeno concocted a number of ingenious arguments to prove that motion is impossible and hence illusory. Now scarcely anyone thought Zeno was right—obviously motion exists! Nevertheless, his paradoxes proved to be most intractable, and philosophers have continued to propose solutions to them right up through the twentieth century.

In the same way, no matter how ingenious the argument, fatalism must be wrong. For it posits a constraint upon human freedom which is altogether unintelligible. The fatalist admits that our decisions and actions may be causally free—indeed,

---

1. Richard Taylor, "Fatalism," *Philosophical Review* 71 (1962): 57; see also his *Metaphysics*, Foundations of Philosophy (Englewood Cliffs, N.J.: Prentice-Hall, 1963), p. 57.
2. Susan Haack, "On a Theological Argument for Fatalism," *Philosophical Quarterly* 24 (1974): 158.

FIGURE 1

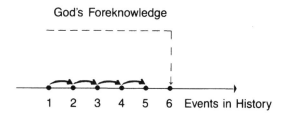

God's Foreknowledge

1 2 3 4 5 6   Events in History

they could be utterly uncaused. Nevertheless, such actions are said to be constrained—but by what? Fate? What in the world is that? How can my action be constrained and my power limited merely by the truth of a future-tense statement about it, especially when my action is causally unconstrained?

Or look at it this way. Suppose God knows that some causally free event will occur. How does his merely *knowing* about it constrain it to occur? Imagine the numbered points in figure 1 represent events in history and the arrows stand for causal connections. Event 6 is causally unconstrained; it can happen or not. Now suppose the broken line represents God's foreknowledge. How does his knowing about event 6 constrain it? Suppose we erase the broken line. The theological fatalist would say event 6 is now not constrained or fated. But what has changed? How does the addition or deletion of the factor of God's simply knowing some act in advance affect the freedom of that act?

Fatalism posits a constraint on human freedom which is entirely unintelligible. Therefore, it must be false. Somewhere there is a fallacy in the argument, and we need only examine it carefully to find the error.

The Fallacy of Fatalism

The three escape routes proposed and rejected in chapter 4 all assumed that divine foreknowledge is in fact incompatible with human freedom. But is this assumption correct? Here and in the next chapter I shall attempt to show that this assumption is wrong.

It will be remembered that I suggested, in explaining Pike's argument, that if one could find a fourth alternative to the three proposed by Pike in step (6), one could escape the threat of fatalism. In fact there is such an alternative, and it has been pointed out and defended by a number of Pike's critics. We may amend Pike's sixth step to read:

6. So if God believed that Jones would mow his lawn on Saturday afternoon, Jones can refrain from mowing his lawn only if one of the following alternatives is true:

    i. Jones has the power to make God's belief false;
    ii. Jones has the power to erase God's past belief;
    iii. Jones has the power to erase God's past existence; or
    iv. Jones has the power to act in a different way, and if he *were* to act in that way, God *would have* believed differently.

We may thus admit that Jones cannot make God's belief false or erase God's past belief or erase God's past existence. But he can do something different (from what he will do) in such a way that God would have held a belief different from the belief he in fact holds. For example, Jones can choose to go golfing on Saturday afternoon instead of mowing his lawn. Now since God foreknows that Jones will mow his lawn, we know that Jones will in fact mow the lawn rather than go golfing. But it does not follow that Jones *must* mow the lawn or that he lacks the power to go golfing. He *can* go golfing, but he merely *will* not. If he *were* to go golfing, then God *would have* foreknown that instead.

This solution is very similar to the one that Pike himself suggests with regard to human foreknowledge of free actions. It will be remembered that, according to Pike, Jones has the power to act in such a way that, if he were to do so, Smith's belief about Jones's action would have been false, though it is in fact true. From the fact that Smith really knows that Jones will mow his lawn, it follows only that Jones *will* mow his lawn, not that he *must* mow his lawn. If he were to refrain, as he is in fact able to do, Smith's actual knowledge would have been just a false belief.

Now Pike thinks this same solution is inapplicable in God's case because Jones does not have the power to act in such a way that God's actual knowledge would have been false belief, since God's knowledge is infallible. Pike is certainly correct that

God's infallibility prevents his holding a false belief. But that same infallibility guarantees that if Jones were to refrain, God would have held a *different* belief. Since God cannot be mistaken or fooled, he would have foreknown from eternity if Jones were going to refrain. God cannot hold a false belief. Therefore, whatever Jones will do, God foreknows it. If Jones were to act differently, God's true belief would not have been false (as in Smith's case); rather his belief would have been different. The solution to the problem is essentially the same in both cases—namely, from Smith's and God's foreknowledge it follows only that Jones *will* act in a certain way, not that he *must* act in that way. If he were to refrain, something that is in fact the case would have been otherwise. The only difference between the two is that Smith's actual knowledge would have been false belief, while God's belief would have been different.

Pike apparently thought that Jones's power to act differently, as envisioned in alternative (iv), meant that Jones has the power to erase God's past belief and to substitute another one for it. But this is a misunderstanding of the alternative. Once God's foreknowledge exists in the past (or present), it is unalterable and immutable. Jones does not have the power to erase God's foreknowledge. Rather alternative (iv) asserts that if Jones *were* to refrain (as he is really able to do), then God *would have* always foreknown differently. Notice the mood of the italicized verbs in the preceding sentence: they are in the subjunctive mood, not the indicative mood. The subjunctive mood serves to indicate that what we have here is a contrary-to-fact hypothetical statement: if something *were* the case (which in fact it is not), then something else *would be* the case. Philosophers call such statements *counterfactual* statements.

From God's foreknowledge that Jones will mow the lawn, we may infer with absolute certainty that Jones will mow the lawn. But he still has the power to refrain. He merely will not exercise that power. If he *were* to refrain (contrary to fact), then God *would have* foreknown that he would refrain. Thus Jones does not have the power to erase God's past belief; rather he has the power to act in a different way, and if he were so to act, God from eternity would have held a belief different from the one he in fact holds.

The reader should now be able to see that the argument for theological fatalism commits a fairly common logical fallacy. In effect the fatalist argues:

Necessarily, if God foreknows x, then x will happen.

God foreknows x.

Therefore, x will necessarily happen.

But such reasoning is universally recognized to be logically fallacious. It is like reasoning:

Necessarily, if Jones is a bachelor, Jones is unmarried.

Jones is a bachelor.

Therefore, Jones is necessarily unmarried.

But Jones is not *necessarily* unmarried. He just *is* unmarried. He is perfectly free to be married; no necessity compels him to be unmarried. The valid form of the argument would thus read:

Necessarily, if Jones is a bachelor, Jones is unmarried.

Jones is a bachelor.

Therefore, Jones is unmarried.

This form of the argument does not preclude that Jones has it in his power to be married. If he were married, then he would not be a bachelor. From the fact that he is a bachelor, we know with absolute certainty that he is unmarried. But he is not necessarily unmarried; that is, it is not impossible for him to be married.

What is impossible is that Jones be both a bachelor and married, for this would be a logical contradiction. But by no stretch of the imagination can we construe Jones's inability to be both a bachelor and married as a limitation on his freedom! What is meant by freedom is that he is free to be either one.

The same situation holds in the case of the argument concerning God's foreknowledge. The valid form of the argument is:

Necessarily, if God foreknows x, then x will happen.

God foreknows x.

Therefore, x will happen.

It is fallacious to infer that x will *necessarily* happen. It just *will* happen. It is entirely possible that x fail to happen. Of course, if it were to fail to happen, God would not have foreknown x. From God's foreknowledge of x we can be absolutely sure that x will occur. But it does not have to occur; it is possible for it to fail to happen.

What is impossible is a situation in which God foreknows x and x fails to happen, for this would be a logical contradiction. It is impossible for both God to foreknow that Jones will mow the lawn and Jones to refrain from mowing the lawn. But by no stretch of the imagination can we construe as a limitation on Jones's freedom his inability to bring about a situation in which both God foreknows that he will mow the lawn and he refrains from mowing it! What is meant by freedom is that Jones is free either to mow or to refrain, and whatever he does God will foreknow.

But it might be protested that if we have an either/or situation in which either God foreknows that Jones will mow the lawn or else Jones refrains, and if God in fact foreknows that Jones will mow, then the other alternative is impossible—Jones cannot refrain! But this objection merely repeats the same fallacy. Jones can refrain, but he simply will not. If he were to refrain, God would not have foreknown that he would mow the lawn.

Perhaps we can make the fallacy of the objection clearer by pointing out why the one alternative is already taken. The fact that Jones will actually mow the lawn is the reason why God foreknows that Jones will mow the lawn. Jones does not mow the lawn because God foreknows; God foreknows because Jones will mow the lawn. Now this does *not* mean Jones's action *causes* God's foreknowledge. The word *because* here indicates a logical, not a causal, relation, one similar to that expressed in the sentence "four is an even number because it is divisible by two." The word *because* expresses a logical relation of ground and consequent. God's foreknowledge is *chronologically* prior to Jones's mowing the lawn, but Jones's mowing the lawn is *logically* prior to God's foreknowledge. Jones's mowing is the ground; God's foreknowledge is its logical consequent; Jones's mowing is the reason why God foreknows that Jones will mow the lawn.

Once we understand the logical priority of the events to God's knowledge of them, we can see more easily why the fact of God's foreknowledge does not prejudice anything. The reason God foreknows that Jones will mow his lawn is the simple fact that Jones will mow his lawn. Jones is free to refrain, and were he to do so, God would have foreknown that he would refrain. Jones is free to do whatever he wants, and God's foreknowledge logically follows Jones's action like a shadow, even if chronologically the shadow precedes the coming of the event itself.

In short, the argument for theological fatalism is simply fallacious. From God's foreknowledge of a free action, one may infer only that that action will occur, not that it must occur. The agent performing the action has the power to refrain, and were the agent to do so, God's foreknowledge would have been different. Agents cannot bring it about both that God foreknows their action and that they do not perform the action, but this is no limitation on their freedom. They are free either to act or to refrain, and whichever they choose, God will have foreknown. For God's knowledge, though chronologically prior to the action, is logically posterior to the action and determined by it. Therefore, divine foreknowledge and human freedom are not mutually exclusive.

Suggested Further Reading

Haack, Susan. "On a Theological Argument for Fatalism." *Philosophical Quarterly* 24 (1974): 156–59.

Plantinga, Alvin. *God, Freedom, and Evil*. Grand Rapids: Eerdmans, 1977. See pp. 66–72.

Davis, Stephen T. "Divine Omniscience and Human Freedom." *Religious Studies* 15 (1979): 303–16.

Wertheimer, Roger. "Conditions." *Journal of Philosophy* 65 (1968): 355–64.

Kim, Jaegwon. "Noncausal Connections." *Noûs* 8 (1974): 41–52.

6

The Necessity
of the Past

Many contemporary theological fatalists recognize that, as it stands, their argument is fallacious. They accordingly try to make the argument valid by making the second step necessary as well as the first:

Necessarily, if God foreknows x, then x will happen.

Necessarily, God foreknows x.

Therefore, x will necessarily happen.

So revised, the argument does not commit the logical fallacy pointed out in chapter 5. For from two necessary premises, a necessary conclusion follows.

That is not to say, however, that the argument is now cogent or correct. For why should we regard the second step as true? If this step is false, then the conclusion is false. And this step, so revised, does seem to be false. Christian theologians have always insisted that the content of God's foreknowledge is not necessary. He could have created a world different from this one or no world at all, in which case his foreknowledge would be different. Necessarily, whatever God knows is true, but it is not necessary that God know what he knows. To say God's foreknowledge is necessary is to say that this is the only world he could have created and that he created it necessarily.

But theological fatalists have a different sort of necessity in mind when they say that God's foreknowledge is necessary.

What they have in mind is the *necessity of the past*. According to them, the past is necessary in a way the future is not. Often this is expressed by saying the past is now unalterable or unpreventable. "Don't cry over spilled milk," we say; or "that's water under the bridge." It is now too late to affect the past, but there is still time to affect the future. In this sense, the past is necessary, while the future is not. And since God's foreknowledge is in the past (since he has *always* foreknown what he foreknows), it is now necessary; it is too late to do anything about it. So then, according to the revised argument of the theological fatalist, the future event *x* is necessary in precisely the same sense: we cannot change or prevent it. Therefore, divine foreknowledge excludes human freedom.

In dealing with this challenge, it seems to me that it is important to distinguish between *changing* the past or future and *causing* the past or future. To change the past would be to bring it about that an event which actually occurred did not occur. To change the future would be to bring it about that an event which actually will occur will not occur. On the other hand, to cause the past would be to produce an event in the past, so that the effect occurs prior to the cause. To cause the future would be to produce an event in the future, so that the effect occurs after the cause. Notice that causing the past or future is not the same as changing the past or future, because in the case of causation the effect is not changed.

Perhaps an illustration can help to make the difference clear. I remember seeing a "Twilight Zone" episode about a little boy who had a deep relationship with a boxer. The prizefighter was involved in the match of his life, and the youngster was watching him on television. To the boy's horror, the boxer lost the match. The little boy fell to his knees and began to pray fervently. Suddenly the scene changed. The boy was now watching the boxer win the match. Through his prayer the boy had managed to *change* the past, so that what had happened had no longer happened.

Let us rewrite the story slightly. Suppose the little boy is unable to watch the fight on television because he was hit by a car and is in a coma at the time of the fight. But on waking up in the hospital room, he sees from the clock on the wall that the fight has probably just ended. He begins to pray fervently that his friend has won the fight. Now suppose that his prayer is answered, so that the prizefighter has won the match because of the prayers of the little boy. In such a case, the little boy has not *changed* the past (since the fighter never lost); rather he has *determined* the past. The effect (winning the fight) simply precedes the cause (the boy's prayers).[1] Thus, causing the past or future does not involve changing the past or future.

Now the issue to be explored here is whether these notions are possible or impossible. Let us begin with the concept of changing the past or future. Changing the past is logically impossible. It is simply self-contradictory to maintain that an event which has occurred has not occurred. To return to our "Twilight Zone" example, God could, in answer to the boy's prayers, make everyone forget that the fighter had lost the match, reconstitute the scene, and play it over again, making sure the second time that the fighter wins. But even God could not bring it about that the fighter never lost in the first place. For it would be self-contradictory to bring it about that a fight which had occurred had not occurred. The unalterability of the past is simply a matter of logic.

But what, then, of changing the future? It is in the same sense just as logically impossible to change the future as the past. For to change the future would be to bring it about that some event which will occur will not occur, which is self-contradictory. As the British philosopher A. J. Ayer explains,

> The past is closed in the sense that what has been has been: if an event has taken place there is no way of bringing it about that it has not taken place; what is done cannot be undone. But it is equally true, and indeed [definitional], that what will be will be; if an event will take place there is no way of bringing it about that it will not take place; . . . for if it were prevented it would not be something that will be done.[2]

---

1. For simplicity's sake, I am assuming here that the prayer itself has somehow caused the past event, rather than that God foreknew the prayer and then acted in normal causal fashion to effect the fighter's victory. This latter case, while having much the same practical implications as backward causation, technically is not backward causation, as we shall see (p. 87).

2. A. J. Ayer, *The Problem of Knowledge* (London: Macmillan; New York: St. Martin's, 1956), p. 189.

Thus, future events are unalterable. But is this not fatalism? Not at all; necessarily, what has been has been and what will be will be. But fatalism holds that what has been has *necessarily* been and that what will be will *necessarily* be. The unalterability of the future does not imply fatalism, for it is just a matter of definition: the future is what will be. According to Ayer, "if [the fatalist's] only ground for saying that an event is fated to occur is just that it will occur, or even that someone knows that it will, there is nothing more to his fate than the triviality that what happens at any time happens at that time, or that if a statement is true it is true."[3] Even Richard Taylor, a fatalist, admits, "All these seemingly grave observations are really utterly trivial, expressing only what is definitionally true."[4] Thus, both the future and the past are unalterable, but unalterability, being merely a definitional truth, has no bearing on fatalism.

What, then, about causing the past or future? Here things do not appear to be the same. On the one hand, while we do not have the power to change the future, we do have the power to cause the future. Moreover, we do so freely. By our present free choices and actions, we help to determine the course of future events. We do not change the future, but we do help to determine what the future will be. It is this ability to cause the future that lies at the root of our idea that the future is open, an idea which is often misexpressed as the power to change the future. Because we have the power, not to change the future, but to cause the future, we have significant freedom.

Do we have a similar power to cause the past? Common sense certainly recoils at such an idea, but it is difficult to show that backward causation is impossible. As we shall see in the next chapter, attempts to show that backward causation is logically impossible have failed. Is backward causation therefore really possible? I think not.

Here we must distinguish between logical possibility and real, or ontological, possibility. Crudely put, something is logically possible if it does not contradict logic. Something is on-

---

3. Ibid., p. 191.

4. Richard Taylor, "Prevention, Postvention, and the Will," in *Freedom and Determinism*, ed. Keith Lehrer (New York: Random House, 1966; Atlantic Highlands, N.J.: Humanities, 1976), p. 73.

tologically possible if it does not contradict being or reality. Certain things may be logically possible but ontologically impossible. For example, it is possible to deny without logical contradiction the statement "whatever begins to exist has a cause." But surely the denial of this statement is ontologically impossible. For it is *really* impossible that without a cause something should spring into being out of nothing. Or consider the statement "no event precedes itself." The denial of this statement would imply a cyclical view of time in which the same moment both precedes and succeeds itself. While there seems to be no logical contradiction in the notion of a cyclical time, such a notion would nevertheless seem to be ontologically impossible, since the repetitions of the cycle would occur one *after* the other, so that a time series of successive cycles of separate events is set up.

But now what about the statement "no effect precedes its cause"? The denial of this statement is logically possible, that is, involves no contradiction. But is the denial *really* possible? I shall argue that backward causation is, indeed, ontologically impossible.

One's view of whether backward causation is ontologically possible seems to be bound up with one's view of time. The commonsense view of time (called the A-theory) holds that temporal becoming is objectively real and that future events do not in any sense exist. Only the events of the present are real; future events are but unactualized possibilities. On the other hand, a good number of scientists and philosophers reject the commonsense view of time. They hold the view (called the B-theory) that the passage of time is purely subjective and events in the future and past are every bit as real as events in the present. The only reason we are in the present is that we are conscious of this particular moment. But people in 1775 and 2075 are conscious of their respective moments as present. There is no privileged present. All moments and events—whether past, present, or future to us—are equally real and existent, and the difference between them is a subjective feature of consciousness.

Now it is no coincidence that virtually all the proponents of backward causation adhere to the B-theory of time. For if past, present, and future events are all equally real and the only difference between them in this respect is purely subjective, it is much easier to imagine how a later event could be the cause of an earlier event. Both events exist; therefore, the earlier event is not caused by some nonexistent future event. As one philosopher of space and time puts it, backward causation rests on the assumption that time is a collection of regions among which our present region is not more real than the others. If one denies this conception of time, he admits, there can be no causal relations across regions of time and hence no backward causation. Thus, "making things to have happened is a package deal with the regional view of time."[5]

By contrast, if the A-theory is correct, backward causation would seem to be ontologically impossible. Since future events in no sense exist, to claim that an event is caused by a future event is to assert that something can come from nothing. For at the time the effect is produced, the future cause is quite literally nothing. And it is ontologically impossible that something should come into existence out of nothing.

The question, then, is which view of time is correct. I hope to explore this issue more fully in a future research project on divine eternity. But for now I shall simply register my opinion that the A-theory captures more adequately the essence of time and that in this regard there is no reason to reject or ignore our commonsense beliefs. As G. J. Whitrow, a philosopher of time, explains, transience belongs to the very essence of time, but this fundamental notion is obscured by the B-theory.[6] The B-theory does seem to be guilty of spatializing time, thus destroying the objective becoming that makes time what it is. I do not see any reason to think that this becoming is purely subjective. B-theorists who are scientists often seem to uncritically assume that their ability to construct a graph or diagram which represents space on one axis and time on the other proves that time is spread out like a line and future things exist. But I see no justification for such an inference. B-theorists who are philosophers often denounce the "myth of the passage of time" ("how fast is time moving?" they ask), but the A-theorist is not committed to

---

5. Graham Nerlich, "How to Make Things Have Happened," *Canadian Journal of Philosophy* 9 (1979): 21.

6. G. J. Whitrow, *The Natural Philosophy of Time*, 2d ed. (Oxford: Clarendon, 1980), p. 372.

saying that time itself moves, but only that events really do elapse or happen one after the other. This position seems not only unobjectionable, but as obvious as any truth perceived by the five senses. I therefore take my stand with the A-theory.

Now if the A-theory is in fact correct, then backward causation is really impossible. We cannot act so as to bring about effects in the past. It is this fundamental difference between the past and the future that accounts for our belief that the past is necessary in a way the future is not. Because we cannot act to affect the past, we think of the past as necessary, a thought we often misexpress by saying the past is unchangeable or unpreventable in a way the future is not.

We have seen that both the past and the future are unchangeable, but that the past is causally closed, whereas the future is causally open. The point to which this rather lengthy analysis has been leading is that *no fatalist has*, to my knowledge, *explained the necessity of the past as anything other than either the unalterability or the causal closedness of the past.* But the unalterability or causal closedness of the past (which includes God's foreknowledge) is either merely a definitional truth or irrelevant to divine foreknowledge; they in no way impose necessity on the content of what God has always foreknown. By contrast, nonfatalists have published studies according to which the necessity of the past is not equivalent to the unalterability or causal closedness of the past, but on these analyses God's foreknowledge inevitably turns out not to be necessary—a conclusion which ruins the fatalist's argument.[7] Fatalists have done little more than facilely appeal to some "fixed past principle" according to which one cannot act in such a way that the past would have been different—but such a principle is an unjustified assumption. The fact is, as we saw in chapter 5, that because we are free and God is omniscient, we do have the power to act in a different way, and were we so to act, the past would have been different in that God's beliefs would

---

7. See the brilliant study by Alfred J. Freddoso, "Accidental Necessity and Logical Determinism," *Journal of Philosophy* 80 (1983): 257–78; see also Thomas P. Flint and Alfred J. Freddoso, "Maximal Power," in *The Existence and Nature of God*, ed. Alfred J. Freddoso (Notre Dame, Ind.: Notre Dame University Press, 1983), pp. 93, 104–7.

have been different. Nonfatalists can therefore concede the unalterability of the past without embracing fatalism, since they do not assert that we have freedom to change the past.

It might be objected that the nonfatalist is committed to backward causation in that God's foreknowledge is the effect and the future event is the cause. But, the objection continues, backward causation is ontologically impossible—God's past beliefs cannot be affected by us and are therefore necessary. We have already seen, however, that the relationship between God's foreknowledge and future events is not causal but logical. Future events do not retroactively cause the thoughts in God's mind. Rather, future-tense statements about future events are true or false depending on how things will turn out. God, being omniscient, has the essential attribute of knowing all true future-tense statements. Therefore, he foreknows the future, even though it is entirely nonexistent. Foreknowledge thus does not require or imply backward causation.

It seems that the fatalists' final gambit has failed. They tried to make their logically invalid argument cogent by making the second step necessary. But we have seen that God's past beliefs are not necessary in any sense that implies fatalism. We think of the past as necessary because we cannot causally affect the past. But our ability to act in such a way that God would have foreknown differently does not involve backward causation. Human freedom and divine foreknowledge are therefore entirely compatible.

Suggested Further Reading

Bradley, R. D. "Must the Future Be What It Is Going to Be?" *Mind* 68 (1959): 193–208.

Whitrow, G. J. *The Natural Philosophy of Time.* 2d ed. Oxford: Clarendon, 1980.

Waterlow, Sarah. "Backwards Causation and Continuing." *Mind* 83 (1974): 372–87.

Freddoso, Alfred J. "Accidental Necessity and Logical Determinism." *Journal of Philosophy* 80 (1983): 257–78.

7

Rejection of Fatalism in Other Fields (1): *Backward Causation*

One of the most fascinating features of fatalism is how often fatalistic reasoning shows up in widely diverse fields. Most philosophers who have discussed theological fatalism seem to be unaware of the studies in these other fields, studies which for the most part reject fatalistic reasoning. This across-the-board rejection of fatalism in its various guises is a powerful confirmation that the argument for theological fatalism is indeed fallacious. Defenders of the biblical view of divine foreknowledge and human freedom can derive support for their position from these other fields in which fatalistic reasoning has been repudiated. In the next four chapters, we shall survey the areas of backward causation, time travel, precognition, and Newcomb's paradox—the reader had better be sure of being firmly buckled into his seat because our exploration of these four fields will take us on flights of fancy that soar far beyond the normal reaches of the human mind!

We begin with the contemporary debate over backward causation, a debate which stems from two articles written by the Oxford philosopher Michael A. E. Dummett—"Can an Effect Precede Its Cause?" (1954) and "Bringing About the Past" (1964).[1] While admitting that it is really or ontologically impos-

---

1. Michael A. E. Dummett and Antony Flew, "Can an Effect Precede Its Cause?" in *Belief and Will*, Aristotelian Society supplementary vol. 28

sible that an effect precede its cause, Dummett argues that backward causation is at least logically possible. He also contends that the argument *against* the logical possibility of backward causation is perfectly parallel to the argument *for* fatalism. Accordingly, these arguments are either both fallacious or both correct.

As his point of departure, Dummett takes a hypothetical example of retrospective prayer. Suppose one hears a radio report that a ship on which one's son is traveling has gone down. Does it make sense to pray now that one's son survived the sinking? Dummett remarks that such a prayer is not asking God to make something happen that did not happen, but asking God to have done something at an earlier time. Retrospective prayer no more asks God to *change* the past (which is logically impossible) than prayer for the future asks him to *change* the future (which is also logically impossible). It asks him only to have done something at an earlier time.

Now the logical objection to retrospective prayer is exactly like the argument for fatalism, asserts Dummett, except that the tenses are different. Those who deny backward causation claim that either the son has already drowned or he has not. If he has drowned, the prayer cannot be answered. If he has not drowned, the prayer is superfluous. So why pray? The fatalist would say the same thing about a future naval disaster: the son will either drown or not drown. If he will, the prayer cannot be answered. If he will not, the prayer is superfluous. So why pray? The two cases are entirely parallel. Since Dummett rejects fatalism, he consistently rejects the logical objection to backward causation as well.

But others, notably Antony Flew, have taken up the defense of the logical objection to backward causation.[2] Flew charges that backward causation would commit us to the contradictory position that what has been done can be undone; if it could not be undone, we would be left with an idea of causation which does not deserve the name, since it would be able to operate only

---

(London: Harrison, 1954), pp. 27–62; Michael A. E. Dummett, "Bringing About the Past," *Philosophical Review* 73 (1964): 338–59.

2. Flew, "Can an Effect Precede Its Cause?" pp. 45–62; see also Antony Flew, in *Encyclopedia of Philosophy*, s.v. "Precognition."

when preceded by its effect. Flew's point is that backward causation involves the logical absurdity of changing the past. If one says that backward causation does not involve changing the past, then one must also say that once the effect has happened, it is impossible to prevent the cause, which is ridiculous. Flew asks us to imagine a "bilking experiment" in which we observe an effect occurring and then afterwards take measures to prevent the cause from operating. If we succeed, we have the absurd situation that the effect is erased from the past; but if we fail, then we are not able to prevent the cause, that is to say, we are not free.

To illustrate Flew's suggested experiment, I recall an amusing story of a professor who had invented a machine that could send objects into the past or future. Gathering his faculty colleagues for a demonstration, the professor placed a cube in the machine and announced, "I shall now send this block five minutes into the future." After adjusting a dial, he pushed a button and at once the cube disappeared. "Where did it go?" asked his astounded colleagues. "Into the future," answered the professor. "In five minutes you shall see it reappear in the machine." Sure enough, five minutes later, the block suddenly appeared in the place it had earlier vacated. "Now," announced the professor with obvious delight, "I shall send the block five minutes into the future. But then I shall send it two minutes into the past. Therefore, in three minutes' time you shall see the block reappear in the machine!" Thereupon he pressed the button again, and again the block disappeared. Three long minutes passed. Suddenly, there was the cube again, sitting in the machine! As his colleagues watched dumbfounded, the professor removed the cube, turning it over in his hand while he waited for two minutes to elapse and the moment to arrive when he should place it into the machine again for its journey into the past. One of his colleagues at that point, however, piped up, "What happens if you don't put it back into the machine?" "Well, I don't really know," confessed the professor, who had never thought of such a thing. "Let's try it and see." Seconds slowly passed as the professor and his colleagues waited for the two minutes to elapse. Whereupon the cube remained where it was, but the machine, the professor, his colleagues, and everything else promptly disappeared!

What may be said in response to the logical objection to backward causation? In the first place, it seems quite clear that Flew mistakenly confused causing the past with changing the past. Since changing the past is, as we have seen, logically impossible, he concluded that backward causation is logically impossible. When Bob Brier, a proponent of backward causation, pointed out to Flew that there is a difference between changing the past and affecting the past and that the latter involves no contradiction,[3] Flew retorted that this distinction between changing and affecting the past is "breathtakingly perplexing." He was "entirely at a loss" to understand Brier's point: "it must be wrong to speak of a present cause bringing about a past effect; since this could only be a matter, either of undoing what has already happened, or of making to have happened what has not happened."[4] But since this distinction was made by Dummett himself in his original article and is common in the literature, Flew's perplexity is itself perplexing. It seems quite clear that if an effect precedes its cause, it has always done so in the sense that the moment in which the effect occurs has never come to pass without the effect's occurring, so that no change in the past is envisioned by backward causation.

Flew contends, however, that if backward causation does not involve changing the past, then it does not deserve the name *causation*, because once the effect has happened, the cause must also occur. But this commits the same logical fallacy as does fatalism. In effect Flew reasons:

Necessarily, if the effect has occurred, then the cause will occur.

The effect has occurred.

Therefore, the cause will necessarily occur.

But this manner of reasoning is logically fallacious, as we have seen. All Flew has a right to conclude is that the cause *will* occur, not that it *must* occur. The cause can still fail to occur,

---

3. Bob Brier, "Magicians, Alarm Clocks, and Backward Causation," *Southern Journal of Philosophy* 11 (1973): 361.

4. Antony Flew, "Magicians, Alarm Clocks, and Backward Causation: A Comment," *Southern Journal of Philosophy* 11 (1973): 365–66.

but in fact it will not (otherwise the effect would not have happened). If the cause were not to happen, neither would the effect have happened.

As for Flew's bilking experiment, it is an implicit endorsement of fatalism. From the effect's occurring, however, it follows only that we *shall* not prevent the cause, not that we *cannot.* If we were to prevent the cause, the effect would not have occurred. To return to our lighthearted illustration, once the professors saw the block appear after three minutes' time, they should have known that two minutes hence the block was not going to be prevented from going back in time—maybe the professor would stumble and accidentally drop the block into the machine, or maybe someone else would place the block in the machine. For if the block were going to be prevented from going back, it would not have appeared after three minutes' time. Remember, the effect's occurring depends entirely on the cause's occurring, so that if the cause were not going to occur, the effect would not have occurred.

It seems, therefore, that backward causation is logically possible. The logical objection to backward causation is, as Dummett noted, exactly parallel to the argument for fatalism and commits the same fallacy. This does not mean that backward causation is really possible. As we saw earlier (pp. 79–81), the nature of time and objective becoming preclude backward causation, even if that notion involves no logical contradiction.

What, then, of retrospective prayer? In the first place, this is not a genuine example of backward causation at all. The prayer itself does not effect something in the past. Rather, God, foreknowing the prayer, brings about something in the present. For example, God, because he foreknows the prayer, has already decided before the shipwreck occurs to save the son when his vessel goes down. Thus, technically, retrospective prayer (just like the truth of future-tense statements and God's foreknowledge based on them) does not involve backward causation, even if such prayer has many of the same practical consequences as does backward causation.

Are we saying that God honors retrospective prayer after all? Philosophically I see no objection to this idea, but that does not mean that God does indeed answer retrospective prayer. The issue is a theological one. I have in fact heard Christians claiming answers to retrospective prayer. A particularly vivid example occurred when Jan and I were working with Campus Crusade for Christ, recruiting students to attend Explo '72, a conference aimed at training a hundred thousand Christians in personal evangelism. In advance of the conference we heard a speaker tell of how God had used the recruitment drive in the lives of the headquarters staff. As the date for Explo '72 drew near, he explained, applications were alarmingly low. Finally, in desperation the leadership and staff came together one weekend for intensive prayer for the conference, which at that point looked as if it were going to be a failure. As they prayed together, they experienced a sort of spiritual revival in their own hearts. And on Monday morning applications began to pour in. The speaker was not dull to the implications. "Those applications had to have been sent by Thursday in order to reach us Monday morning," he explained. "Therefore, God, foreknowing that we were going to pray, had already answered in advance, so that the response to our prayers came immediately!" Coincidence? I do not know. Jesus said, in teaching his disciples to pray, "Your Father knows what you need before you ask him" (Matt. 6:8)— but he did not say that God answers prayer prior to its being offered. On the other hand, perhaps Jesus had in the back of his mind the promise of Isaiah 65:24: "Before they call I will answer, while they are yet speaking I will hear." The answer clearly precedes the prayer; but even so, there is no suggestion here that we should pray for the past. As far as I know, the Scripture neither enjoins nor gives any example of prayer for the past. This issue must then, I suppose, be settled by individual Christian conscience.

Suggested Further Reading

Dummett, Michael A. E. "Bringing About the Past." *Philosophical Review* 73 (1964): 338–59.

Brier, Bob. *Precognition and the Philosophy of Science: An Essay on Backward Causation.* Atlantic Highlands, N.J.: Humanities, 1974.

8

Rejection of Fatalism in Other Fields (2): *Time Travel*

We now turn to one of the most fascinating and mind-boggling areas in which arguments parallel to fatalism arise: time travel. Scientists and philosophers agree that the sort of time travel envisioned by H. G. Wells in his famous novel *The Time Machine* is in fact impossible. Since Wells's machine moved only through time but not through space, it would, so to speak, run into itself as it journeyed back and forth in time. With the development of Albert Einstein's Special Theory of Relativity, however, time travel emerged as a new possibility if the time traveler moves through space as well as through time. In 1949 the mathematical genius Kurt Gödel proposed a model of the universe in which all matter is involved in a cosmic rotation. The most incredible feature of this model is that it permitted the existence of "time loops," so that by taking a sufficiently wide curve a space traveler in a rocket ship could journey into any region of the past or future and return. Unfortunately for time-travel buffs, the universe apparently lacks the cosmic rotation necessary for time travel, so that such journeys are in fact impossible. As G. J. Whitrow explains, the evidence supports instead the existence of a cosmic time which originated with the big bang.[1]

---

1. G. J. Whitrow, *The Natural Philosophy of Time*, 2d ed. (Oxford: Clarendon, 1980), p. 307.

Nevertheless, some philosophers are not content to rest simply with the physical impossibility of time travel. They argue also that time travel is logically impossible, that it involves a self-contradiction. Many of their objections are clearly parallel to the fallacious reasoning of fatalism. Gödel himself, for example, worried that if his model were correct, a man might travel into the past, meet himself, and do something to himself that he knows did not happen to him, since his memory does not recall it. Such a worry is groundless, however. From the fact that the man does not remember his time-traveling self's having done something to his past self, it follows only that either the time-traveling self will not do anything to the past self or else the man's memory is faulty in not remembering what happened. If we assume that his memory is accurate, it does not follow that the time traveler *cannot* do something to his past self, but only that he *will* not. If he were to do something, he would remember it.

David Lewis suggests a more complex scenario.[2] Suppose the time traveler goes back in time and kills his grandfather before he has any children. If the time traveler were to do this, he himself would never have been born so as to travel into the past on his murderous mission. But killing his grandfather seems very easy for the time traveler to do: all he has to do is pull the trigger once he has his grandfather in his sights!

In response to Lewis, one cannot reply as one did to Gödel: from the fact that the time traveler exists, it follows only that he *did* not kill his grandfather, not that he *could* not kill his grandfather; but if he were to kill his grandfather, then the time traveler would not exist. This response, as I say, makes no sense at all, for in order to kill his grandfather he has to exist. And therein lies the fallacy of the objection. Lewis is asking the time traveler to perform a logically absurd task. Killing one's grandfather before he has any children is an inherently unintelligible act. But the possibility of time travel in no way implies the possibility of such an absurd task. A proponent of time travel will insist that the time traveler cannot perform such an action. For such an action would be equivalent to changing the past,

2. David Lewis, "The Paradoxes of Time Travel," *American Philosophical Quarterly* 13 (1976): 151.

that is, bringing it about that the grandfather both has and has not produced children. But time travel does not entail an ability to change the past, but merely the ability on the part of the future to have shaped the past, at least to some extent. It is not therefore time travel itself which is unintelligible, but the task which the time traveler is asked to perform. Thus, no one need lose any sleep over the worry, "What if my son should come from the future and kill me before I have children?" On the other hand, if time travel is possible, one could conceivably be troubled by the fear, "What if my son should come from the future and kill me after I beget him?"

Fatalistic reasoning crops up once again in another objection to time travel, namely, that time travel could result in a self-inhibiting situation. Imagine a rocket ship equipped with a probe which can travel along time loops into the past. Suppose also that the rocket ship is programed to fire the probe only if a safety switch is turned off. If the switch is on, the probe will not be fired. Suppose furthermore that the rocket ship is equipped with a sensing device to detect the return of the probe. If the device detects the probe returning, it automatically turns the safety switch on. If the probe is not detected, the switch remains off. Now the question is, Is the probe fired or not? If the returning probe is detected, the sensing device turns the switch on, so that the probe will not be fired. But if the probe is not detected, the switch is left off, so that the probe will be fired. Thus, if the probe is fired, it is not fired, and if it is not fired, it is fired. Time travel thus results in a logically self-inhibiting situation.

Now this argument admittedly does not prove that time travel per se is impossible; rather, the whole scenario is impossible. One could avoid the absurdity by rejecting some feature of the situation other than the time loops (e.g., the possibility of building the sensing device). But theorists who deny the possibility of time travel maintain that we have good grounds for affirming the physical possibility of the other aspects of this scenario; hence the possibility of time loops must be rejected.

Persuasive as this reasoning might at first appear, it commits the same fallacy as does the reasoning in support of theological fatalism. As Paul Horwich points out, in a world in which time loops exist it may be possible for the rocket and its equipment (probe, safety switch, sensing device) to exist—just as long as the rocket and its equipment never *in fact* exist and function properly.[3] Those who deny the possibility of time travel fallaciously infer that in a universe in which time loops exist, the rocket and its equipment *cannot* exist and function properly, when all they have the right to infer is that the rocket *will* not exist and function properly. The proponent of time travel maintains that if the rocket were to exist and function properly, then the time loops would not exist. What is impossible is that *both* the time loops exist *and* the rocket and its equipment exist and function properly. From the existence of time loops, argues the proponent of time travel, it follows only that the rocket will not exist and function properly, not that it cannot.

I must confess that when compared with our position on God's foreknowledge of future events, this response by the proponent of time travel leaves me with a great deal of discomfort. For there seems to be a crucial difference between the case of divine foreknowledge and the case of time travel. In the former case the future event is the ground of the foreknowledge, that is, the foreknowledge is determined by the event; but in the latter case the existence of the time loops is totally unrelated to the existence of the rocket, that is, the rocket and its equipment do not determine the structure of space and time. Therefore, it would seem that if the existence and proper functioning of such a rocket is even possible in a world in which time loops exist, then a self-inhibiting situation is possible, which is absurd.

To provide an analogy, consider the statements "Lincoln was assassinated" and "I have it in my power to eat ice cream." It seems undeniable that if I were to eat ice cream, then it would be true both that Lincoln was assassinated and that I eat ice cream. This is because Lincoln's death is totally independent of my eating ice cream, so that it is not affected by my action. In a similar way, the existence of time loops is totally independent of the existence and proper functioning of the rocket. Accordingly, if the latter were to exist, then it would be true both that time loops exist and that the rocket exists and functions properly, which results in a self-inhibiting situation. Thus, if time loops exist, the possibility of the rocket implies the possibility of an

---

3. Paul Horwich, "On Some Alleged Paradoxes of Time Travel," *Journal of Philosophy* 72 (1975): 440.

absurdity. Since such machines are physically possible, time loops must be physically impossible if absurdity is to be avoided.

Now cogent as this reasoning seems, it is in fact fallacious. For there is a crucial difference between the case of Lincoln and the ice cream and the case of time travel. In the former case there is no contradiction between Lincoln's assassination and my eating ice cream, but in the latter case it is *logically impossible* for both the time loops to exist and the rocket to exist and function properly. It therefore follows that if the loops exist, the rocket does not; if the rocket exists and functions properly, then the loops do not exist. Both *cannot* be true. There is no possible world containing both. But it *is* possible to have a world in which one exists and the other is merely possible, for example, a world in which time loops exist and the rocket is merely possible. One need only add that were the rocket to exist and function properly, then the time loops would not exist. This is *not* to say the structure of space and time depends on the working of such machines. Not at all; it is just that it is logically impossible for the two to exist together. To demand why the rocket and its equipment are never built or function properly in any possible world in which time loops exist is, as Horwich says, merely to ask why contradictions do not come true.

The proponent of time travel would thus seem to be vindicated. In a world in which time loops exist, it is not the case that the rocket cannot exist, but only that it will not exist or function properly. For the two are logically incompatible. If the rocket were to exist and function properly, then the time loops would not exist—not, indeed, because the existence of the loops depends on the working of such machines, but simply because contradictions are not possible.

The failure of the logical objection to time travel lends further support to the position that divine foreknowledge and human freedom are compatible. Just as the existence of time loops would imply only that the rocket will not exist, not that it cannot exist, so the existence of divine foreknowledge of a free action implies only that that free action will take place, not that it must take place. And just as it is true that if the rocket were to exist, then the loops would not, so it is true that if the free action were to be different, then God's foreknowledge would have been different. Indeed, the case for time travel can be even more instructive in this regard, for if God is conceived to be not just inerrant, but essentially infallible (i.e., not only does he make no mistakes, but it is logically *impossible* for him to be mistaken), then even in the absence of any ground-consequent relationship between a future event and God's foreknowledge of it, it would be true that were the event not to occur, God would not have foreknown it. For it is logically impossible that God should believe that some event will occur and that event not occur; there is no possible world in which God's beliefs are mistaken. But we have seen that the case of divine foreknowledge is even more plausible than the case of time travel, for in the former case the occurrence of the future event determines what God foreknows. Hence, it is all the more obvious that were it not to occur, God would not have foreknown its occurrence.

Does all of this mean that time travel is really possible as well? No, for time travel, like backward causation, presupposes the B-theory of time and is therefore ontologically impossible.[4] If the past and future do not exist, it is impossible to travel to them. In addition to this general point, however, I think it can be shown that time travel implies the possibility of a vicious sort of circular causation. Consider a case in which the time traveler encounters himself in the past. Suppose that during this meeting the time traveler gives to his earlier self the plans for building the time machine and that this is his only source of information. The earlier self later uses the plans to build the machine. He then travels into the past to give the information to his earlier self. Thus the later self knows how to build the machine because he remembers what the earlier self learned, but

---

4. Proponents of time travel explicitly endorse the B-theory of time. Imagining a time traveler who journeys from 1978 to 3000 B.C. to help the Egyptians build the pyramids, Larry Dwyer remarks, "All phenomena exist in a four-dimensional world known as spacetime. . . . The world line of the time traveller and his rocket lie (tenselessly) in spacetime. . . . We must resist the tendency to think that between 3000 B.C. and 1978 the fact of the time traveller's arrival in ancient Egypt and his pyramid building activities are in some sense 'harder' facts than his subsequent construction of a rocket and successful take-off in 1978." ("Time Travel and Some Alleged Logical Asymmetries Between the Past and Future," *Canadian Journal of Philosophy* 8 [1978]: 17, 29; cf. Lewis, "Paradoxes of Time Travel," p. 146).

the earlier self learned it from the later self. So where did the information come from? Such circular causation is not logically impossible, but it clearly is, I think, really impossible.

Perhaps the wildest example of such circular causation I have encountered concerns the time traveler who journeys into the past and marries his mother, thus becoming his own father! Not only that, he then journeys further into the past, has a sex-change operation, and later marries himself, so that he turns out to be not only his own father, but his own mother as well![5] If time travel were possible, such an absurd scenario would be possible. Therefore, time travel, like backward causation, even if logically possible, appears to be really impossible.

Suggested Further Reading

Horwich, Paul. "On Some Alleged Paradoxes of Time Travel." *Journal of Philosophy* 72 (1975): 432–44.

---

5. Robert Heinlein, "All You Zombies," in *The Best from Fantasy and Science Fiction*, ed. Robert P. Mills (New York: Ace, 1958). I am indebted to William Hasker, not only for this reference, but also for several very stimulating discussions on the contents of this chapter.

9

Rejection of Fatalism
in Other Fields (3):
Precognition

We begin to approximate very closely the issue of divine foreknowledge when we turn to the third area of inquiry in which parallels to fatalistic reasoning exist: the parapsychological phenomenon of precognition. Parapsychological studies fall into two divisions: extrasensory perception (ESP) and psychokinesis. Psychokinesis is the influencing of a physical object by the mind without physical intermediaries. ESP may be subdivided into the three categories of clairvoyance, telepathy, and precognition. Clairvoyance and telepathy involve supernormal cognition of contemporaneous events, while precognition is cognition of future events.

Although many philosophers and scientists regard precognition as utter nonsense, the evidence for it is impressive. One thinks, for example, of the experiments conducted by Whately Carrington at Cambridge in the late 1930s.[1] At seven o'clock on ten successive evenings Carrington hung in his study a sketch of some object. The sketch remained on the wall until half past nine the next day. In the meantime, persons in various countries tried to reproduce the sketch via telepathy. The results of the experiment failed to show any telepathic perception of the

---

1. Whately Carrington, "Experiments on Paranormal Cognition of Drawings," *Proceedings of the Society for Psychical Research* 46 (1940–1941): 34–151; 46 (1941): 277–340; 47 (1944): 155–228.

drawing hanging on the wall. Curiously, however, there did turn out to be a remarkable resemblance between the reproductions and the sketches which Carrington had hung the previous two evenings and which he was to hang the subsequent two evenings. Although the subjects of the experiment could not reproduce the drawing hanging on the wall on a given evening, they displayed a noteworthy accuracy with regard to the two previous and two subsequent drawings, an accuracy which Carrington calculated would result by chance in only one case out of ten thousand. There thus appeared to be good evidence for precognition, for Carrington did not determine the subject of the drawing until just before seven o'clock each evening and he did so by a random procedure. He opened a book of mathematical tables, picked the last digits of the first two or three groups of numbers he saw, turned to the corresponding page of a dictionary, and then selected the first appropriate word on that page as the subject to be sketched—a procedure which made prediction by inference impossible.

Even more remarkable were the card-guessing experiments conducted by S. G. Soal.[2] At first nothing in the results of his experiments with 160 persons suggested that correct guesses were anything more than mere chance. But in 1939 Carrington, after publishing his findings, urged Soal to reexamine his case studies to see if there might be similar phenomena of retro- or precognition. Soal reluctantly reexamined his records and to his amazement discovered that two of his subjects did indeed display a pattern of accurate guessing with regard to the preceding and subsequent card. Soal then carried out further experiments with each of these two subjects, those with Basil Shackleton continuing for two years. In these experiments cards depicting five different animals were used. As a "telepathic agent" looked at the cards in a random order, Shackleton would, at a signal, guess which animal the agent was looking at. Soal used thirteen different telepathic agents and found that with three of them

2. S. G. Soal, "Fresh Light on Card-Guessing—Some New Effects," *Proceedings of the Society for Psychical Research* 46 (1940–1941): 152–98; S. G. Soal and K. M. Goldney, "Experiments in Precognition Telepathy," *Proceedings of the Society for Psychical Research* 47 (1943): 21–150; S. G. Soal and F. Bateman, *Modern Experiments in Telepathy* (London: Faber and Faber, 1954).

there were significant results in regard to the card the agent was to view next. With two of these agents, Shackleton correctly guessed the next card 28.95 percent of the time. This does not seem to be a very high percentage, especially when one realizes that by chance alone one would guess correctly 20 percent of the time. Nonetheless, the difference of 8.95 percent in a total of 5,799 attempts represents a deviation so significant that the odds of its occurring by mere coincidence are one in 2.4×10^{63}! C. D. Broad, an eminent British philosopher who became intrigued with the possibility of and evidence for precognition, concluded that although the percentage of Shackleton's correct guesses was not very high, it was still so persistent as to rule out chance:

> It is so persistent that the odds against so strong an association persisting as a mere chance-coincidence, in a run of guesses so long as that actually made, are colossal. They are such as to rule out that hypothesis completely. It is for this reason that we say that the results of these experiments seem *prima facie* to establish the occurrence of "precognition" on the part of Mr. Shackleton.[3]

More-recent experiments have relied on electronic devices to present and randomize the targets to be guessed. In the experiments of H. Schmidt, for example, the subjects were instructed to press a button to indicate which of four colored bulbs they thought would light next.[4] An electronic switch which designated each bulb 250,000 times every second determined which one lit up after the button was pressed. Between the pressing of the button and the closing of the switch there was a delay of approximately a tenth of a second. The precise length of the delay was determined by the random decay of a piece of radioactive strontium 90. It was clearly impossible to infer which bulb would light next. In one experimental run of 63,066 guesses, three subjects exceeded chance by a little over 690 correct selections—the odds of such a result are five hundred

---

3. C. D. Broad, "The Notion of Precognition," *International Journal of Parapsychology* 10 (1968): 167.

4. H. Schmidt, "Precognition of a Quantum Process," *Journal of Parapsychology* 33 (1969): 99–108.

million to one. In another series of twenty thousand guesses, four subjects were asked to indicate which bulb they thought would *not* light. The results were so significant that the odds of their occurring by chance were ten billion to one. Similar results were obtained by E. F. Kelly and B. K. Kanthamami, using Schmidt's machine to test a gifted subject.[5] R. Targ and D. B. Hunt ran similar experiments with a ten-year-old girl who was so successful that the odds against her obtaining such results by chance were 10^{15} to one![6] On the basis of these and similar experiments, one might conclude that the evidence is sufficiently strong to establish the existence of human precognition.

Some philosophers, however, have denied the possibility of precognition of chance events or free decisions. J. L. Mackie of Oxford University asserted that Flew's bilking experiment is "fatal" to precognition of such events, for once the precognition has occurred, one could prevent the precognized event from occurring.[7] The error of Mackie's reasoning should be clear by now. From the fact that the precognition has occurred, it follows only that the precognized event *will* occur, not that it *must* occur or cannot be prevented. If some person precognizes what picture will be hung on the wall tomorrow, it follows that that picture will be displayed. For some reason or other, the experimenter's attempt to prevent it will go awry—perhaps an uninformed lab assistant or the janitor will hang up the picture. For if the hanging of the picture were prevented, the subject would not have precognized it—there would have been either no cognition at all or else a cognition which was merely an erroneous guess. If, on the other hand, a genuine precognition of a future event does occur, all that we have the right to infer is that the event will take place, not that it will take place necessarily.

This failure of the fatalistic objection to precognition of a free event lends additional support to the defender of divine foreknowledge and human freedom. For precognition is simply the

5. E. F. Kelly and B. K. Kanthamami, "A Subject's Efforts Toward Voluntary Control," *Journal of Parapsychology* 36 (1972): 185–97.

6. R. Targ and D. B. Hunt, "Learning Clairvoyance and Precognition with an ESP Teaching Machine," *Proceedings of the Parapsychological Association* 8 (1971): 9–11.

7. J. L. Mackie, *The Cement of the Universe* (Oxford: Clarendon, 1974), p. 176.

parapsychological analogue for the theological term *foreknowledge*. Philosophers studying parapsychology have recognized that the fatalistic objection provides no cogent reason for rejecting the compatibility of precognition and human freedom; why cannot theologians see the same?

Does this mean that human precognition is therefore possible or likely? It all depends on whether precognition presupposes backward causation. Philosophers such as C. D. Broad and C. W. K. Mundle rightly argue that precognition based on backward causation is impossible because of the nature of time.[8] Since both of them adhere to the A-theory of time, they reject backward causation; if, therefore, precognition requires backward causation, it, too, must be rejected.

In this connection, Broad distinguishes between two types of objection to a retrocausal account of precognition: an *epistemological* objection and an *ontological* objection. The epistemological objection concerns the knowledge of a future thing; the ontological objection concerns the being of a future thing. Broad maintains that while the epistemological objection is incorrect, the ontological objection is correct.

According to the epistemological objection, precognition of a future thing is impossible because the precognized object does not exist. In other words, one cannot foreknow what does not exist. Broad notes that this objection rests on two assumptions, both of which he considers wrong: (1) that precognition is of the nature of perception, so that it is quite literally preperception of a future thing; and (2) that ordinary perception involves direct acquaintance with the perceived object. Broad rejects (1) because such a model of precognition would also eliminate memory, since memory would be postperception. If preperception is impossible, then so is postperception, since past things no more exist than do future things. But it is absurd to say memory is impossible. Against (2), Broad argues that we do in some cases have perceptions of events which do not exist, as when we hear a

---

8. C. D. Broad, "The Philosophical Implications of Foreknowledge," in *Knowledge and Foreknowledge*, Aristotelian Society supplementary vol. 16 (London: Harrison, 1937), pp. 199–200; idem, "Notion of Precognition," pp. 190–93; C. W. K. Mundle, "Does the Concept of Precognition Make Sense?" *International Journal of Parapsychology* 6 (1964): 187–89.

gunshot a mile away. When we hear the shot, the actual firing no longer exists.

I do not find Broad's rejection of the second assumption very convincing,[9] but his argument against the first assumption seems quite correct:

> It is very doubtful whether any precognitive experience is *literally* pre-perception of the event or state of affairs which will in due course fulfill it. And precognition, insofar as it is not literally of the nature of perception, is *epistemologically* on all fours with ordinary non-inferential retro-cognition, which admittedly presents no particular epistemological difficulty.[10]

Broad thinks that memory is in fact a better model of precognition than is perception. Once one rejects the construal of precognition in terms of perception, the fact that the future does not exist presents no epistemological difficulty. Antony Flew agrees:

> One consequence which has often been thought to follow from the existence of precognition is that, sensationally, the future must somehow be already here—or at any rate there. This is usually derived from a conception of precognition as a mode of perception, of extrasensory perception. . . .
>
> It is inconceivable that anyone should be able to see things which do not yet exist. Nevertheless, the correct conclusion is not . . . that precognition is logically impossible. The correct conclusion is, rather, that if the phenomenon specified was to occur, it could not be conceived of as any sort of perception.[11]

It seems to me that Flew's conclusion is correct: precognition is not perception and therefore does not depend upon the future's already existing.

By contrast the ontological objection is deemed by Broad to be truly a problem for the retrocausal account of precognition.

---

9. We do have direct acquaintance with the traces of the perceived past event. Therefore, the perceptual model of precognition justifiably assumes that foresight of the future requires direct acquaintance.

10. Broad, "Notion of Precognition," p. 190.

11. Antony Flew, in *Encyclopedia of Philosophy*, s.v. "Precognition."

According to the ontological objection, a precognition cannot be *caused* by a future thing, for the future does not exist. Broad, who originally held to the B-theory of time but came to embrace the A-theory, maintains that it is plainly nonsensical to say that a future event sets up a chain of effects and causes going backward in time and eventually resulting in the precognitive experience. For until the future event happens, nothing can be caused by it, since the future event *is* nothing but an unrealized possibility until it comes to pass.

Broad's analysis of the ontological objection seems quite correct: the retrocausal account of precognition must be rejected. We are led to the conclusion that if precognition is based on backward causation, then precognition is ontologically impossible. The question is not settled so easily, however, since precognition does not have to appeal to backward causation as its basis. One could adopt, for example, a model of the Platonic theory of recollection in order to explain precognition. According to Plato, souls existed before they were united with their bodies in the world, and in this preincarnate state they possessed innate knowledge. When placed into their respective bodies, however, souls forgot the knowledge they possessed in their preincarnate condition. According to Plato, education consists in helping the soul to recollect the knowledge it innately possesses but has forgotten. Education is therefore in Plato's view not really learning or *acquisition* of knowledge, but rather *recollection* of innately possessed knowledge. Now a defender of precognition could adopt such a model of precognition, maintaining that the mind possesses subconsciously an innate knowledge of certain future events and that in a few gifted individuals this knowledge has at least partially risen to consciousness. I do not mean to suggest that this provides a plausible account of the phenomenon of precognition; my point is merely that precognition does not necessarily imply backward causation and that, therefore, the ontological impossibility of backward causation does not serve to settle automatically the issue of the possibility of precognition.

It would seem therefore that the question of whether human precognition exists must be settled simply by the evidence. Telepathy, clairvoyance, and chance could explain many or most cases of alleged precognition, though explaining away one parapsychological phenomenon by another raises a whole new set of questions. However the issue may be finally judged, the important lesson we have learned is that the same fatalistic reasoning that has been urged against the compatibility of divine foreknowledge and human freedom has been judged to be fallacious by those working in the realm of precognitive phenomena.

Suggested Further Reading

Gauld, Alan. "ESP and Attempts to Explain It." In *Philosophy and Psychical Research,* edited by Shivesh C. Thakur, pp. 17–45. Muirhead Library of Philosophy. London: Allen and Unwin; Atlantic Highlands, N.J.: Humanities, 1976.

Broad, C. D. "The Philosophical Implications of Foreknowledge." In *Knowledge and Foreknowledge,* pp. 177–209. Aristotelian Society supplementary vol. 16. London: Harrison, 1937.

———. "The Notion of Precognition." *International Journal of Parapsychology* 10 (1968): 165–96.

Mundle, C. W. K. "Does the Concept of Precognition Make Sense?" *International Journal of Parapsychology* 6 (1964): 179–98.

Scriven, Michael. "Randomness and the Causal Order." *Analysis* 17 (1956–1957): 5–9.

10

Rejection of Fatalism in Other Fields (4): *Newcomb's Paradox*

The closest analogy to divine foreknowledge of human free decisions comes in the realm of decision theory and concerns a puzzle called Newcomb's paradox. Originally the brain-child of William Newcomb of the Lawrence Livermore Laboratory (University of California), this puzzle was passed on to the philosophical public by Harvard University's Robert Nozick in 1969.[1] I shall try to explain the puzzle as simply as possible.

Imagine a television game show in which the contestant—let us call her Joan—is presented with two boxes, B_1 and B_2. Joan may choose to have the contents either of B_2 alone or of both B_1 and B_2 together. She is informed that B_1 contains $1,000. Now the game show employs an individual who is enormously successful in predicting the contestants' choices; in fact, he has never made an incorrect prediction. The hitch is this: If he predicts Joan will choose both boxes, he leaves B_2 empty. But if he predicts that Joan will choose B_2 alone, he puts $1,000,000 in B_2.

Now what should Joan do? According to Nozick there are two very plausible arguments which lead to different decisions:

---

1. Robert Nozick, "Newcomb's Problem and Two Principles of Choice," in *Essays in Honor of Carl G. Hempel*, ed. Nicholas Rescher, Synthese Library (Dordrecht: D. Reidel, 1969), pp. 114–46.

1. Joan might reason, "If I take what is in both boxes, then the predictor will almost certainly have made a prediction to this effect and left B_2 empty. But if I take B_2 alone, then he will have made a prediction to that effect and put the $1,000,000 in B_2. So I shall take B_2 alone!"

2. Or Joan might reason, "The $1,000,000 is either already sitting in B_2 or it is not; that is already fixed and determined. If the predictor has already put the $1,000,000 in B_2 and I choose both boxes, then I'll get $1,001,000. If he has not, then I'll get $1,000. Either way I'll get $1,000 more than I would by taking B_2 alone."

Nozick seeks to strengthen the force of each of these arguments. With regard to the first argument, he invites us to suppose that all previous contestants who chose B_2 alone got the $1,000,000. All the clever ones who followed the reasoning of the second argument wound up with only $1,000. It would be a very safe bet for some third person to wager that if Joan chooses both boxes, she will get only $1,000. In fact, Joan herself ought to offer such a bet to members of the studio audience!

With regard to the second argument, Nozick asks us to suppose that B_1 is transparent so that Joan can see the $1,000 sitting there. Moreover, the $1,000,000 is either already in B_2 or it is not. Should she choose only what is in B_2? Suppose, further, that B_2 has a transparent side facing the audience, who can thus plainly see whether B_2 is empty or not. The money is not going to miraculously appear or disappear. Moreover, whether B_2 is empty or full, the audience is hoping that she will take both boxes. For if B_2 is empty, they want Joan to get at least the $1,000 in B_1, and if B_2 is full, they want her to get not only the $1,000,000, but the $1,000 as well. With a little reflection Joan must know what the audience is hoping. Should she then choose only B_2, thus passing up the $1,000 which she can plainly see and ignoring the silent hopes of every member of the audience that she choose both?

In the face of these two conflicting arguments, what should Joan do?

Nozick originally presented the paradox as a dilemma for decision theory, but the paradox has obvious relevance to the problem of theological fatalism which we are considering. For it is natural to identify the predictor with God and to take the paradox as an illustration of the problem of divine foreknowledge and human freedom. In fact, Nozick himself later approved of the identification of the predictor with God.[2]

Certain philosophers have argued that Newcomb's paradox thus shows that divine foreknowledge destroys free will. Maya Bar-Hillel and Avishai Margalit assert that the predictor's success proves that one's feeling of free choice between the boxes is an illusion: "Although the facts really imply that there is no free choice, the illusion of free choice persists, and you can do no better than to behave as if you do have free choice."[3] Similarly, Don Locke asserts,

> Once the Predictor has made his prediction, that prediction becomes fixed and unalterable: having made the one prediction, it is no longer possible for him to make the other. So given that the Predictor is absolutely infallible, it is at the time of choosing equally impossible, and in just the same sense, for the chooser to make any choice other than that predicted.[4]

According to Locke, the infallible accuracy of the predictor "gives me every reason to think that I have no choice in the matter at all, or that if I do have any freedom it is a freedom I am unlikely to exercise."[5]

On the other hand, George Schlesinger thinks that the fatalistic implications of Newcomb's paradox succeed in showing that an infallible and omniscient predictor cannot exist.[6] In the same way, a gleeful Isaac Asimov proclaims,

> I would, without hesitation, take both boxes. . . . I am myself a determinist, but it is perfectly clear to me that any human being

2. Robert Nozick, cited in Martin Gardner, "Mathematical Games," *Scientific American*, March 1974, p. 102.

3. Maya Bar-Hillel and Avishai Margalit, "Newcomb's Paradox Revisited," *British Journal for the Philosophy of Science* 23 (1972): 302.

4. Don Locke, "How to Make a Newcomb Choice," *Analysis* 38 (1978): 21.

5. Ibid., p. 23.

6. George Schlesinger, *Aspects of Time* (Indianapolis: Hackett, 1980), pp. 79, 144.

worthy of being considered a human being (including most certainly myself) would prefer free will, if such a thing could exist. ... Now, then, suppose you take both boxes and it turns out (as it almost certainly will) that God has foreseen this and placed nothing in the second box. You will then, at least, have expressed your willingness to gamble on his nonomniscience and on your own free will and will have willingly given up a million dollars for the sake of that willingness—itself a snap of the finger in the face of the Almighty and a vote, however futile, for free will. . . . And, of course, if God has muffed and left a million dollars in the box, then not only will you have gained that million, but *far more important* you will have demonstrated God's nonomniscience.[7]

Unwilling to abandon either divine foreknowledge or human freedom, Dennis Ahern concludes from Newcomb's paradox that the problem of foreknowledge and freedom is unresolvable.[8] For it is unreasonable to believe, on the one hand, that a person can have control over God's past beliefs, since backward causation is impossible. But it is equally implausible to believe, on the other hand, that a free action becomes nonfree simply because it is foreknown or predicted. But if one of these statements is false, then the other must be true; they both look false, but they both cannot be false. Hence, the situation is inherently paradoxical.

What may be said in response to these varied reactions to Newcomb's paradox? Well, Ahern's conclusion may be dismissed right away. If he is correct, the assumption of divine foreknowledge and human freedom leads to a logical absurdity. Therefore, one must deny either that an omniscient God exists or that human beings are free. But this is precisely the position of the other philosophers we have mentioned. The question, then, is whether those critics are correct that Newcomb's paradox proves the incompatibility of God's foreknowledge and human freedom.

Perhaps the best way to get at this problem is to return to the dilemma as Nozick presented it for decision theory. Nozick maintained that Newcomb's paradox brings into conflict two

---

7. Isaac Asimov, quoted in Gardner, "Games," p. 104.
8. Dennis M. Ahern, "Foreknowledge: Nelson Pike and Newcomb's Problem," *Religious Studies* 15 (1979): 489.

principles for decision making which have been enunciated by decision theorists: the *Expected Utility Principle* and the *Dominance Principle*. According to the Expected Utility Principle, a person confronted with a decision should select the option which can be expected to bring the greatest personal benefit. According to the Dominance Principle, if one is confronted with a choice in which one alternative is better than the other, no matter how other things in the world may be, then one should pick that alternative.

Table 1 shows the various possibilities in the situation we are considering. According to the Expected Utility Principle, for each of Joan's choices we should estimate the probability of either A or B being the case, multiply that figure by the dollar amounts involved, and then add the results for A and B together. For example, suppose Joan chooses (i). The probability of God's having predicted that Joan would choose B_2 alone is high, say 90 percent. That means the chance of column B's being the case if Joan chooses (i) is only 10 percent. So we multiply $1,000,000 × .90 and $0 × .10 and add the results together to get $900,000. Now suppose Joan chooses (ii). The odds of column B's being the case are 90 percent and column A only 10 percent. So we multiply $1,001,000 × .10 and $1,000 × .90 and add the results together to get $101,000. Comparing the expected utility of action (i) to that of action (ii) makes it clear that Joan should choose (i).

On the other hand, the Dominance Principle tells us that if the world is divided into two states and a particular choice is better in one state and at least equal in the other, then we should take that choice. For then we cannot lose. Now in table 1 the world is divided into states A and B, and choice (ii) is better in both states. Whether A or B is the case, Joan gets $1,000 more than if she were to take choice (i). Thus, Newcomb's paradox

TABLE 1. **Newcomb's Paradox**

Predictions / Choices	(A) God predicts that Joan will choose B_2 alone	(B) God predicts that Joan will choose B_1 and B_2
(i) Joan takes B_2 alone	$1,000,000	$0
(ii) Joan takes B_1 and B_2	$1,001,000	$1,000

seems to bring the two principles of decision theory into conflict with each other.

A number of philosophers, however, have pointed out an apparent fallacy in this reasoning. In order for the Dominance Principle to apply, each of the states (A and B) must remain equally probable whether one chooses alternative (i) or (ii). That is to say, whether one chooses (i) or (ii), the probability of A remains the same, and likewise for B. Philosophers call this requirement "probabilistic independence." The fallacy in our example is that A and B are not probabilistically independent. For if Joan chooses (i), then state A is overwhelmingly more probable than B, and if she chooses (ii), then state B is vastly more probable than A. The probabilities change with the choices. Therefore, the Dominance Principle is inapplicable, and one must follow the recommendation of the Expected Utility Principle.

Nozick has, however, a rejoinder to this objection. He furnishes a counterexample in which the Dominance Principle applies even though the states of the world are not probabilistically independent of the choices taken. Suppose a young man named Tom does not know whether Smith or Walker was his real father. Both men are now dead. Smith died of a hereditary disease, but Walker did not. If Smith was Tom's father, then Tom will die of this disease; but if Walker was his father, then he will not. Now this disease has the peculiar side effect of making a person intellectually inclined. Tom is trying to decide whether to go to graduate school in philosophy or to become a baseball player, and he slightly prefers the academic life.

TABLE 2. **Nozick's Counterexample**

Heredity / Choices	(A) *Smith is Tom's father*	(B) *Walker is Tom's father*
(i) Tom goes to graduate school	Tom is briefly a philosopher and then dies (−20)	Tom is a philosopher and has a normal life-span (+100)
(ii) Tom plays baseball	Tom is briefly a baseball player and then dies (−25)	Tom is a baseball player and has a normal life-span (+95)

Table 2 outlines the possible outcomes of Tom's choices and assigns a preference value to each. If he follows the Dominance Principle, Tom will choose (i), because whether state A or B is the case, this option is preferable. But then he probably has the disease, since one of its symptoms is to be intellectually inclined. On the other hand, if he follows the Principle of Expected Utility, he will choose (ii). But this choice, says Nozick, is "perfectly wild." Although state B is more probable if Tom chooses (ii), the fact is that whether A or B is the case is already determined and does not depend on Tom's choice. Tom's choice can in no way affect whether Smith or Walker was his father. By choosing (ii), Tom cannot make it less likely that Smith was his father or less likely that he has the disease.

Nozick concludes, "In situations in which the states, though not probabilistically independent of the actions, are already fixed and determined, where actions do not affect whether or not the states obtain, then it *seems* that it is legitimate to use the Dominance Principle."[9]   But he adds that even then "the crucial fact is *not* whether the states are already fixed and determined, but whether the actions *influence* or *affect* which state obtains."[10] In any case in which such influence exists, one should always use the Principle of Expected Utility.

Nozick's analysis provides the key to unlocking the puzzle of Newcomb's paradox when God is the predictor. The reader will recall that in the original statement of the paradox, Joan's choice had absolutely no influence on the predictor's forecast. That is to say, contrary to the impression given by several writers, the original predictor in Newcomb's paradox did not make his predictions on the basis of precognition. In its original formulation, Newcomb's paradox is analogous to Tom's situation in deciding whether to go to graduate school or to become an athlete: the choices have no influence at all on which state of the world is actual. The predictor's forecasts were just incredibly lucky guesses.

But once the predictor is identified with God, the picture changes completely. For God's prediction is based on precognition of the choice or, in the language of theology, on foreknowl-

---

9. Nozick, "Newcomb's Problem," p. 127.
10. Ibid., p. 132.

edge. In this case, the actions do affect which state of the world is actual, for what one chooses determines what God predicts, since his predictions are based on his foreknowledge of one's actions. Hence, Nozick concedes,

> If one believes that the way the predictor works is by looking into the future, [that] he, in some sense, sees what you are doing, and hence is no more likely to be wrong about what you do than someone else who is standing there at the time and watching you, and would normally see you, say, open only one box, then there is no problem. You take only what is in the second box.[11]

In fact, Alvin Plantinga points out that in the case of divine foreknowledge, there is a logically demonstrative argument for choosing only one box:[12]

If Joan were to choose B_1 and B_2, then God would have believed that she would choose B_1 and B_2.

If Joan were to choose B_1 and B_2 and God believed that she would do so, then God would not have put any money in B_2.

Therefore, if Joan were to choose B_1 and B_2, then God would not have put any money in B_2.

A parallel argument proves that if she were to choose B_2 alone, then God would have put the $1,000,000 in B_2. Hence the only rational choice is for her to choose B_2 alone.

Such a solution does not appeal to any sort of backward causation. Nozick acknowledges that he used terms such as "influence" and "affect" without much concern for technical precision.[13] We have seen in previous chapters, however, that in the case of divine foreknowledge such words should not be interpreted in terms of causation, but rather in terms of the logical priority of the events to the content of what God knows. Since certain future-tense statements are true by virtue of the way

---

11. Ibid., p. 134.
12. Alvin Plantinga, "Ockham's Way Out," *Faith and Philosophy* 3 (1986): 256.
13. Nozick, "Newcomb's Problem," p. 146.

things eventually turn out, and God, being omniscient, knows all true future-tense statements, his knowledge of the future is logically determined by how things will turn out.

Moreover, it should be noted that if we believe that God is not simply inerrant (does not make a mistake), but also infallible (cannot possibly make a mistake), then the choice of B_2 alone is correct even if one has no influence at all over God's predictions. For if he is infallible, it is logically impossible for him to be mistaken. Therefore it is logically impossible for Joan to get $1,001,000. It is equally impossible to get $0. For these outcomes can result only if the predictor makes a mistake. The choice then is simply between $1,000,000 and $1,000, and it takes no genius to figure out which of these options to choose!

If God is infallible, then what we have is a situation analogous to the time-travel scenario in which it is impossible for both the time loops and the rocket to exist (and function properly). The existence of the time loops does not depend on the rocket; nevertheless, if the rocket were to exist and function properly, the loops would not exist. Similarly in the case of an infallible predictor: even in the absence of any determining influence, if Joan were to choose other than she will, the predictor would have made a prediction to that effect, for it is logically impossible for him to be mistaken.

What, then, of Nozick's arguments for choosing both boxes? The fact that the money already either is or is not in B_2 should not affect Joan's choice. For even if there is no money in B_2, it is still true that if Joan *were* to choose B_2 alone, then there *would be* $1,000,000 in B_2. As for the audience, if they sufficiently understand the situation, then upon seeing the money in B_2, they will rejoice that Joan is going to choose B_2 alone; or upon seeing no money in B_2, they will regret that Joan is about to make the mistake of choosing both boxes. A moment's glance informs the audience what Joan will do, so that hoping that she will choose B_2 alone is an inappropriate reaction.

This does not mean that Joan is not free to make either choice. There is no constraint on her freedom whatsoever. Whatever she chooses, God will have foreknown. She determines by her free choice what God has foreknown and predicted. God's foreknowledge entails only what she *will* do, not what she *must* do. As one philosopher nicely puts it, "The player is free—he just cannot escape being 'seen' making his free choice."[14]

Newcomb's paradox thus serves as a vivid illustration of the compatibility of divine foreknowledge and human freedom. Joan is free to choose whatever she wants and her choice logically determines what God foreknows. From the fact of God's prediction, we may validly infer only what Joan will choose; we may not infer that she is not free to choose otherwise. With the vindication of the choice of B_2 alone, the death of theological fatalism seems ensured.

Let us pause at this point to review the argument of part 2, in which we tried to show the compatibility of divine foreknowledge and human freedom. Having presented the basic argument for fatalism, we saw that the problem is not unique to theology, but confronts anyone who holds that certain future-tense statements about free acts are true. The denial of the truth of such statements is groundless and springs from a misunderstanding of the notion of truth as correspondence. On the other hand, there are good reasons to affirm that certain future-tense propositions are true; indeed, the denial of such an affirmation leads to absurd consequences. The claim that statements are timelessly true provides no way of escape from the threat of fatalism. Christian theologians thus find themselves in the company of almost all philosophers in trying to combat this threat.

We saw that the reasoning for fatalism, however engaging, must be false because fatalism is simply unintelligible. It posits a constraint on decisions which are causally unconstrained and therefore free. But this mysterious constraint has never been identified and explained by any fatalist.

We then showed that fatalistic reasoning is in fact logically fallacious. The fatalist fails to understand counterfactual statements concerning one's freedom to do other than what one in fact will do. Such freedom does not mean that one has the power to erase the past, but that one has the power to act in a different way, and if one *were* to so act, then God's past foreknowledge would always have been different. Although God's foreknowl-

---

14. James Cargile, "Newcomb's Paradox," *British Journal for the Philosophy of Science* 26 (1975): 237.

edge is chronologically prior to the events foreknown, the events are logically prior to God's foreknowledge of them. This is not to say that the events backwardly cause thoughts to exist in God's mind. Rather, since future-tense propositions are true or false depending on how things will turn out, and God knows all true future-tense propositions, it follows that were one to act differently, God would have foreknown differently.

The attempt to render the fatalist's reasoning valid by appealing to the necessity of the past is fruitless. What the fatalist means by the necessity of the past is the unalterability or causal closedness of the past. But such notions are useless to the fatalist, since the future is as unalterable as the past, and divine foreknowledge is not based on backward causation. God's foreknowledge, though past, is not necessary, for we have the power to act in a different way, and were we so to act, God would have foreknown differently.

The fallacies of fatalism have been exposed not only in the fields of logic and philosophy of religion, but also independently in studies concerning backward causation, time travel, precognition, and Newcomb's paradox. These areas illustrate with increasing proximity the failure of theological fatalism. What a tragedy it would be if Christian theologians, who are usually deficient in their grasp of philosophy, were, because of their lack of philosophical acumen and their ignorance of the repeated failure of fatalistic reasoning in various other fields, to embrace it in the field of theology, thus denying the scriptural truth of divine foreknowledge and human freedom!

Suggested Further Reading

Nozick, Robert. "Newcomb's Problem and Two Principles of Choice." In *Essays in Honor of Carl G. Hempel,* edited by Nicholas Rescher, pp. 114–46. Synthese Library. Dordrecht: D. Reidel, 1969.

Gardner, Martin. "Mathematical Games." *Scientific American,* March 1974, pp. 102–9.

Ahern, Dennis M. "Foreknowledge: Nelson Pike and Newcomb's Problem." *Religious Studies* 15 (1979): 475–90.

Horgan, Terence. "Counterfactuals and Newcomb's Problem." *Journal of Philosophy* 78 (1981): 331–56.

————. "Newcomb's Problem: A Stalemate." In *Paradoxes of Rationality and Cooperation*, edited by Richmond Campbell and Lanning Sowden, pp. 223–34. Vancouver: University of British Columbia Press, 1985.

Brams, Steven J. *Superior Beings*. New York: Springer-Verlag, 1983.

PART 3

The Basis
of Divine Foreknowledge

11

Innate Knowledge

Those who deny divine foreknowledge, having failed to show that it is incompatible with human freedom, very often regroup and turn for a second wave of assault: there is no *way* for God to know future free acts. For it is impossible to infer such events from present causes. How then can they be known? Even if it is true that foreknowledge would not be incompatible with human freedom, still it does not seem possible for God to have such knowledge.

In dealing with this objection, it is important to remember that the burden of proof lies on the objector, who must prove that divine foreknowledge is impossible. The Christian may quite correctly say, "I do not in fact know how God foreknows future free decisions. But why *should* I know how God has such foreknowledge? Who are human beings that they should know how God foreknows the future? Unless there is some reason to think that such foreknowledge is impossible, it is perfectly rational to believe in it." In other words, all the Christian has to show is that such foreknowledge has not been proved to be impossible, that there is no good reason to reject it. The Christian cannot be expected to explain the *actual* way that God foreknows future free events; all the Christian has to do is suggest some *possible* way.

Why should we think that it is impossible for God to know future free decisions? The opponent of foreknowledge would probably respond that future events (1) do not exist, since temporal becoming is objective, and (2) cannot be inferred from present causes, since they are assumed to be free. Therefore, it is impossible for God to know future free events.

119

Now this reasoning makes a couple of assumptions that need to be brought to the forefront. In the first place, it assumes that the A-theory of time is correct. For if the B-theory were right, one could maintain that God, being timeless and spaceless, transcends the entire space-time universe and perceives it as a whole. All of time is stretched out before him, and he in his timeless existence thus knows all events. Or if one wished to place God in time, one could maintain that the basis of divine foreknowledge is a sort of backward causation by means of which future events retroactively cause cognitions of themselves in God's mind. Or one could hold that God's consciousness travels forward in time to view the events of the future at their respective times, and thus he foreknows them. On the B-theory of time, then, one could propose several bases for God's foreknowledge of the future.

I am, however, inclined to grant that the A-theory is correct. I therefore regard any theory of divine foreknowledge presupposing the B-theory of time as ontologically impossible. The question, then, is whether divine foreknowledge of free acts is possible on the A-theory of time.

The second assumption underlying this objection to divine foreknowledge is that all genuine knowledge is based on either immediate perception or causal inference. But why should we accept this assumption? What proof is there that *all* genuine knowledge is based on either immediate perception or causal inference? In fact, does not experience teach us to the contrary that much of our knowledge is acquired neither by sense perception nor by causal inference? Consider our knowledge of ethical values or principles, for example. We do not know right and wrong by means of sense perception or causal inference, yet this is genuine knowledge.

Perhaps the opponent of foreknowledge would adjust the assumption to say that all genuine *informative* knowledge of the empirical world is based on immediate perception or causal inference. But what about one's knowledge that other minds besides oneself exist? Philosophers have shown that there is no way one can prove that other people are not just animals or automata that act as if they have minds but in fact do not. The reader might well respond that only some crackbrained philosopher could entertain such a belief—but that would be missing the point. Nobody believes that other minds do not really exist; the point is that our knowledge that other minds exist is not based on immediate perception of those minds or causal inference, and yet it is genuine knowledge.

In any case, how do we know that the heavy reliance which we as embodied persons have on perception and causal inference would apply to an infinite disembodied Mind? Obviously God does not have knowledge based on sense perception (since he has no sense organs). So could he not possess all knowledge wholly apart from causal inferences as well?

In a very helpful article, Edward Khamara points out that the question of the basis of divine foreknowledge is usually approached from either of two angles: the empiricist or the rationalist.[1] The empiricist approach tends to interpret God's foreknowledge on the model of perception, whereas the rationalist tends to interpret it in purely conceptual terms. According to Khamara, interpreting foreknowledge on the model of perception tends to construe God as an omniperceiver. Thus, one would speak of God's "foreseeing" the future or his "foresight" of some event to come. But Khamara contends that the perceptual model runs into the problem that it apparently cannot provide God with knowledge of the past or future, for the idea of literally perceiving the past or future does not make sense. We have already seen in our discussion of human precognition (pp. 101–2) that such misgivings concerning the perceptual model are entirely justified. So then, the empiricist approach does not offer an adequate model for divine foreknowledge. Indeed, I should go as far as to say that *the implicit assumption of the perceptual model underlies virtually all contemporary denials of the possibility of divine foreknowledge of free acts.*

But what about the rationalist approach to divine foreknowledge? This approach denies that all genuine knowledge is based on either immediate perception or causal inference. The rationalist approach construes divine foreknowledge on a conceptualist model. God innately knows only and all true

---

1. Edward J. Khamara, "Eternity and Omniscience," *Philosophical Quarterly* 24 (1974): 212–18.

statements. Since true future-tense statements are included among them, he foreknows the future.

A conceptualist model can come in different forms. One could maintain that God's knowledge of future-tense statements is simply innate and logically foundational. Or one could maintain that God's knowledge of future-tense statements is based on logically prior statements which he knows and which enable him to know the truth of future-tense statements. This latter form of the conceptualist model has a name of its own: middle knowledge. It is so important that it deserves a separate chapter. For now, though, the question is whether a conceptualist model which holds that God simply knows only and all true statements is possible.

Once we free ourselves from the assumption of the perceptual model implicit in the objection to divine foreknowledge, there is no problem: a conceptualist model is certainly *possible*. And that is all the Christian needs to show in order to turn back the force of the objection to foreknowledge.

In fact, it is fascinating that such a model has even been proposed as an explanation of human precognition. Taking his cue from Jungian psychology, Alan Gauld suggests that extrasensory perception, including precognition, does not occur at all; rather the mind possesses innately such knowledge on a subconscious level, and on occasion this knowledge surfaces in consciousness. He explains,

> The term ESP is a complete misnomer. We do not acquire the factual knowledge exhibited in so-called ESP by any quasi-perceptual or transmissive process, though sometimes we may fancy we do because of the form in which it manifests. The knowledge concerned is, from the point of view of our everyday notion of how we acquire factual information, totally anomalous. The knowledge is not "acquired," the information does not "arrive." The knowledge, so to speak, "happens." "However incomprehensible it may appear," writes Jung, "we are finally compelled to assume that there is in the unconscious something like an *apriori* knowledge or immediate presence of events which lacks any causal basis."[2]

---

2. Alan Gauld, "ESP and Attempts to Explain It," in *Philosophy and Psychical Research*, ed. Shivesh C. Thakur, Muirhead Library of Philosophy

Once we rid ourselves of the perceptual model, we can "stop worrying in connection with precognition about the problem of 'future causes' and all that goes with it."[3] Whether or not such an approach can adequately explain precognition, it does provide a very attractive account of divine foreknowledge. God never learned or acquired his knowledge, but has eternally known an innate store of only and all true statements. Since future-tense statements are either true or false, God in knowing all true statements knows the future.

The opponent of foreknowledge might persist in demanding, "But *how* can God have innate knowledge of all future-tense statements?" The intent of this question, however, is not clear. It cannot mean, "How did God acquire such knowledge?" for it is said to be innate. Nor do I think the question means, "How is the concept of innate knowledge possible?" for the concept does not appear to be incoherent. Perhaps the question really means, "How is it the case that God has innate knowledge?" But then the question appears to be merely an expression of incredulity which requires no answer. God simply is that way, just as he is also omnipotent, necessary, morally perfect, and so forth. The only answer is that God has the essential property of knowing only and all true statements. That is part of what it means to be God, to be omniscient. And to ask how it is that God is omniscient is like asking how it is that vacuums are empty.

The opponent of foreknowledge might raise one final objection. Granted that God possesses by nature only and all true beliefs, still these beliefs do not deserve to be called *knowledge.* For knowledge is not merely true belief—there has to be some justification for what one believes. For example, suppose I believe that on April 2, 1802, Napoleon spat in a puddle, and suppose that this belief is true. Do I therefore *know* this? No, for I have no grounds for my belief. My true belief is more like a correct guess than knowledge. Similarly, God has no justification for his beliefs about the future. They may all be true, but

(London: Allen and Unwin; Atlantic Highlands, N.J.: Humanities, 1976), p. 36. The quotation from C. J. Jung is from *Synchronicity* (London: Routledge & Kegan Paul, 1972), pp. 43–44.

3. Ibid., p. 37.

they are more like incredibly lucky guesses than true knowledge.

This objection may strike us as somewhat perverse. "If our definition of knowledge implies that a being who holds only and all true beliefs and does so infallibly cannot be said to have 'knowledge,' then so much the worse for our definition of knowledge!" the Christian might exclaim indignantly. Such a reaction would be entirely appropriate philosophically. In fact, epistemologists are well aware of the inadequacy of the definition of knowledge as "justified true belief," and have proposed various alternative definitions and accounts of justification. For example, Robert Nozick suggests that a person—let us use the designation P—knows x if and only if the following conditions are met:

1. P believes x;
2. x is true;
3. if x were false, P would not believe x; and
4. if x were true, P would believe x.[4]

Now clearly, on this account, God's true beliefs do count as knowledge, for he believes all true statements and believes no false statements and does so infallibly. My point is not that Nozick's account of knowledge is the one we ought to adopt, but simply that objections to divine omniscience which are based on current definitions of knowledge are very tenuous and therefore not very impressive.

That point aside, however, surely God is justified in holding his true beliefs. Consider, for example, God's true belief that "in A.D. 1984 William Mallory John Craig will be born." Did God have adequate justification for this belief when the world began? Of course he did, for also among his store of beliefs was the belief "God holds only and all true beliefs." Since the former belief is among the beliefs God holds, it must be true. In knowing himself to be God, God knows that all the beliefs he holds are true. But how, it might be asked, does he know that he is God? Certainly not by inference from other facts. He knows that he is

---

4. Robert Nozick, *Philosophical Explanations* (Cambridge: Harvard University Press, Belknap Press, 1981), pp. 172–78.

God simply by immediate self-acquaintance. This sort of knowledge is like our knowledge of personal identity. I know that I am myself simply by acquaintance.

It should now be evident that the opponent of foreknowledge has been no more successful in attempting to show that divine foreknowledge is impossible than in attempting to show that such foreknowledge is incompatible with human freedom. Once one jettisons the unjustified and implausible assumption that all genuine knowledge is based on immediate perception or causal inference, no objection remains to embracing a conceptualist model of divine foreknowledge. One version of such a model, presented here, holds that God possesses innate knowledge of all true future-tense statements. If such a model is even *possible*, then the Christian can reasonably hold to the doctrine of divine foreknowledge of future free acts. The attempt to construe God's knowledge as unjustified true belief is unavailing, for there is no consensus among epistemologists as to exactly what constitutes justification of true belief, and, furthermore, God surely by his immediate awareness that he is God and thus knows only and all true statements has justification for his beliefs.

Suggested Further Reading

Khamara, Edward J. "Eternity and Omniscience." *Philosophical Quarterly* 24 (1974): 204–19.

Suppe, Frederick. "Afterword—1977." In *The Structure of Scientific Theories*, 2d ed., edited by Frederick Suppe, pp. 716–28. Urbana: University of Illinois Press, 1977.

Lewis, David. "Attitudes *De Dicto* and *De Se*." *Philosophical Review* 88 (1979): 513–43.

12

Middle Knowledge

Although the version of the conceptualist model of divine foreknowledge considered in chapter 11 is entirely sufficient to turn back objections to the possibility of such knowledge, another version of the conceptualist model penetrates even more deeply into the structure of divine knowledge. It proposes to explain God's foreknowledge on the basis of middle knowledge, a kind of knowledge that is logically prior to foreknowledge. First suggested by Jesuit theologians of the sixteenth century, middle knowledge, if coherent, is one of the most fruitful theological ideas ever conceived. For it would serve to explain not only God's knowledge of the future, but divine providence and predestination as well.

Explanation of Middle Knowledge

Logical Priority

In order to understand the concept of middle knowledge, it is imperative that we first understand the concept of logical priority. This is a very subtle notion, especially in the context of middle knowledge. To say that something is logically prior to something else is *not* to say that the one occurs before the other in time. Temporally, they could be simultaneous. Rather, logical priority means that something serves to explain something else. The one provides the grounds or basis for the other. For example,

127

the premises in an argument are logically prior to the conclusion, since the conclusion is derived from and based on the premises, even though temporally the premises and conclusion are all simultaneously true.

We have already encountered the difference between logical and temporal priority in our discussion of divine foreknowledge (p. 74). There, it will be recalled, we saw that while God's foreknowledge is chronologically prior to future events, nonetheless the future events are logically prior to divine foreknowledge. One could also correctly say that the future events are logically prior to the truth or falsity of statements about them, since these statements are true or false on the basis of how the events turn out. Accordingly, the logical order is quite different from the chronological order:

Logical Order	Chronological Order
1. Certain events occur.	1. Statements about certain future events are true or false, and of these statements God knows only and all those that are true.
2. Statements about these events are true or false.	2. The events occur.
3. Of these statements God knows only and all those that are true.	

Chronologically, certain future-tense statements are true from the beginning of time and are simultaneously known by God; later on, the events corresponding to these statements occur. Logically, God foreknows the events because certain future-tense statements about them are true, and such statements are true because the events will occur.

Accordingly, just as we talk about temporal moments, so can we speak of logical moments. Logically, in the first moment certain events occur; in the second moment statements about them are true or false; and in the third moment God knows only and all the true statements. The moment at which an event occurs is logically prior to the moment at which God knows about it. Now, clearly, this does not mean that there was a *time* at which certain events occurred without God's knowing about them. The priority here is purely logical, not temporal.

Three Moments in God's Knowledge

Now the proponents of the concept of middle knowledge maintain that there are likewise three logical moments in God's knowledge. Of course, temporally there are no distinct moments in God's knowledge, for everything he knows he knows simultaneously. Logically, however, there is a certain structure to God's knowledge, and some aspects of his omniscience are prior to others.

In the first moment is God's knowledge of all necessary truths, for example, the laws of logic. God does not make such statements true by willing them to be true (indeed, this first logical moment precedes any decision or decree of the divine will). Rather, statements which are true in this moment are true by virtue of the nature of God himself and so do not depend on his will. He knows them to be true by his very nature, and so this first moment of divine knowledge is called *natural knowledge*. God's natural knowledge includes knowledge of all possibilities. He knows all the possible individuals he could create, all the possible circumstances he could place them in, all their possible actions and reactions, and all the possible worlds or orders which he could create. God could not lack this knowledge and still be God; the content of God's natural knowledge is essential to him.

To skip ahead, the third moment of God's knowledge is his knowledge of the actual world which he has created. This includes his foreknowledge of everything that will happen. The third moment is logically posterior to God's decision to create the world. Therefore, he has control over which statements are true and which are false in this moment. By willing to create another world, God would have brought it about that statements which are in fact true would be false and statements which are in fact false would be true. For example, if God had created a world in which George Washington never existed, then all the true statements about things he did would be false. Thus, which statements are true and which are false in the third moment depends on the free decision of God as to which world he has willed to create. Accordingly, this third moment of knowledge is called *free knowledge*. It is God's knowledge of the actual world. God could lack this knowledge and still be God. He must

have this *sort* of knowledge to be God, but its *content* could be
different. For if he had created a different world, the content of
his free knowledge would be different.

In between God's natural knowledge and his free knowledge,
in the second moment of omniscience, stands God's *middle
knowledge*. In this moment God knows what every possible
creature *would* do (not just *could* do) in any possible set of
circumstances. For example, he knows whether Peter, if he were
placed in certain circumstances, would deny Christ three times.
By his natural knowledge God knew in the first moment all the
possible things that Peter *could* do if placed in such circumstances. But now in this second moment he knows what Peter
would in fact freely choose to do under such circumstances.
This is not because Peter would be causally determined by the
circumstances to act in this way. No, Peter is entirely free, and
under the same circumstances he could choose to act in another
way. But God knows which way Peter *would* freely choose.
God's knowledge of Peter in this respect is not simple foreknowledge. For maybe God will decide not to place Peter under
such circumstances or even not to create him at all. Middle
knowledge, like natural knowledge, thus is logically prior to the
decision of the divine will to create a world.

In this second moment of knowledge, God knows which of
the possible worlds known to him in the first moment are
within his power to create. For if it is true that Peter would sin if
placed in certain circumstances, it follows that even though a
world with identical circumstances in which Peter does not sin
is possible, nevertheless it is not within God's power to create
that world. For if he were to create such circumstances and place
Peter in them, then Peter would sin. This does not mean that
God could not prevent Peter's sinning, for he could; but then the
circumstances would no longer be *identical* because God would
be interfering. Hence there are any number of possible worlds
known to God in the first moment of knowledge which he cannot create because free creatures would not cooperate. His middle knowledge serves, so to speak, to delimit the range of
possible worlds to those he could create, given the free choices
which creatures would make in them.

God's middle knowledge is like his natural knowledge in that
it is logically prior to his decision to create a world. Indeed,

Table 3. **The Three Logical Moments of God's Knowledge**

1. *Natural Knowledge:* God's knowledge of all possible worlds. The content of this knowledge is essential to God.
2. *Middle Knowledge:* God's knowledge of what every possible free creature would do under any possible set of circumstances and, hence, knowledge of those possible worlds which God can make actual. The content of this knowledge is not essential to God.

God's Free Decision to Create a World

3. *Free Knowledge:* God's knowledge of the actual world. The content of this knowledge is not essential to God.

God's decision to create a world is based on his middle knowledge and consists in his selecting to become actual one of the possible worlds known to him in the second moment. But middle knowledge is like his free knowledge in that its content is not essential to God. Since creatures could choose differently, God's knowledge would be different if they were to do so.

The three logical moments in God's knowledge are summarized in table 3. It is important to emphasize again that temporally there are no such successive moments in God's knowledge. His decision to create the world is an eternal decision; there never was a time when God had middle knowledge but lacked free knowledge. Table 3, then, shows merely the logical structure of God's knowledge, making clear how each type of knowledge logically presupposes the preceding type(s).

The Biblical Evidence of Middle Knowledge

Why suggest that God has middle knowledge? Basically, two sorts of considerations come into play here: biblical and theological. The sixteenth-century theologians felt that they had good biblical grounds for ascribing middle knowledge to God. One of the texts most often cited was 1 Samuel 23:6–13:

> When Abiathar the son of Ahimelech fled to David to Keilah, he came down with an ephod in his hand. Now it was told Saul that David had come to Keilah. And Saul said, "God has given him into my hand; for he has shut himself in by entering a town that has gates and bars." And Saul summoned all the people to war, to

go down to Keilah, to besiege David and his men. David knew
that Saul was plotting evil against him; and he said to Abiathar
the priest, "Bring the ephod here." Then said David, "O LORD, the
God of Israel, thy servant has surely heard that Saul seeks to come
to Keilah, to destroy the city on my account. Will the men of
Keilah surrender me into his hand? Will Saul come down, as thy
servant has heard? O LORD, the God of Israel, I beseech thee, tell
thy servant." And the LORD said, "He will come down." Then
said David, "Will the men of Keilah surrender me and my men
into the hand of Saul?" And the LORD said, "They will surrender
you." Then David and his men, who were about six hundred,
arose and departed from Keilah, and they went wherever they
could go. When Saul was told that David had escaped from Keilah, he gave up the expedition.

This story was understood to show that God knew that if David
were to remain at Keilah, then Saul *would* come to get him, and
that if Saul *were* to come to get David, then the men of the city
would hand him over. For if God's answers through the ephod
are taken as simple foreknowledge, we must conclude that his
answers were false, since what was predicted did not happen.
But if the answers are understood as indications of what would
happen under certain circumstances, then they were true and
serve as proof of God's middle knowledge.

A second passage commonly appealed to was Matthew
11:20–24:

Then [Jesus] began to upbraid the cities where most of his mighty
works had been done, because they did not repent. "Woe to you,
Chorazin! woe to you, Bethsaida! for if the mighty works done in
you had been done in Tyre and Sidon, they would have repented
long ago in sackcloth and ashes. But I tell you, it shall be more
tolerable on the day of judgment for Tyre and Sidon than for you.
And you, Capernaum, will you be exalted to heaven? You shall be
brought down to Hades. For if the mighty works done in you had
been done in Sodom, it would have remained until this day. But I
tell you that it shall be more tolerable on the day of judgment for
the land of Sodom than for you."

Here Jesus himself declares that if his miracles *had been* per-
formed in certain cities which did not in fact repent, they *would
have* repented. Taken literally, what Jesus is saying here is that

under certain circumstances certain individuals would have acted in a particular way. This was taken as a positive proof of his divine middle knowledge.

Theological Ramifications

Beyond the biblical evidence the Jesuits saw that theological capital was to be gained by ascribing middle knowledge to God. Prescience, providence, and predestination could be explained in a manner compatible with human freedom.

Prescience, or foreknowledge, is beautifully explained on the dual basis of middle knowledge and the divine will. Here we pick up the loose thread from the previous chapter. Middle knowledge is a form of the conceptualist model of divine fore-knowledge. It holds that God did not acquire his knowledge of the future by "foreseeing" what lay ahead. Rather he has such knowledge innately. Nonetheless, foreknowledge is not log-ically foundational, but is based on God's logically prior middle knowledge and his free decision to create a world. By his middle knowledge God knows all the various possible worlds which he could create and what every free creature would do in all the various circumstances of those possible worlds. For example, God knew that Peter, if he were to exist and be placed in certain circumstances, would deny Christ three times. By a free deci-sion of his will, God then chose to create one of those possible worlds. Knowing both every possible world he could create and his decision to create one of them, God foreknows exactly what will happen, that is to say, he has foreknowledge. Knowing, for example, that Peter would deny Christ three times under cer-tain circumstances and knowing his own decision to bring about those circumstances, God knows what Peter will in fact freely do. Thus, God is able to know future free acts on the basis of his middle knowledge and his creative will.

If it be asked how God has middle knowledge of free decisions by creatures, proponents of middle knowledge usually respond in one of two ways: (1) God by his infinite understanding knows each creature so completely that he discerns even the creature's free decisions under any conceivable circumstance. Since the moment of middle knowledge is logically prior to God's cre-ation, no actual creatures exist at that moment, but God comprehends them as they exist in his mind as possible creatures. He knows them so well that he knows what they would freely do in any situation. (2) Statements about how creatures would decide to act if placed in certain circumstances are true or false; since God is omniscient, he knows all truth; therefore, God simply knows all true statements about how creatures would act in certain circumstances. This explanation is essentially the same as our arguments for divine foreknowledge in chapter 11, except here it is applied to middle knowledge, and foreknowledge is accounted for on the basis of God's middle knowledge.

It might seem that foreknowledge, explained in this way, smacks of a divine "sting operation"—it could sound as though God manipulates people by leading them into situations in which they are induced to act in a certain way, even if freely, and thus God knows what they will do. Such an understanding is, however, needlessly unsympathetic. Two truths must be kept in mind: (1) God is a gracious, loving God, not a manipulative tyrant. He loves his creatures and wants the best for them. We may trust in the wisdom of his decision concerning which world to create. (2) In the circumstances in which people find themselves, they are genuinely free to choose opposite courses of action. That God knows what they will do in any set of circumstances does not mean that they are compelled by the circumstances to do what they do. God does not determine their choice; they can choose freely between alternative courses of action. It is God's will and desire, moreover, that they always choose for the good.

Besides, divine foreknowledge without prior middle knowledge would be exceedingly strange. Without middle knowledge, God would find himself, so to speak, with knowledge of the future but without any logically prior planning of that future. To see the point, imagine that logically prior to the divine decision to create a world, God has only natural knowledge. If creatures are going to be genuinely free, then God's creation of the world is a blind act without any idea of how things will actually be. True, he knows at that prior moment all possible worlds, but he has virtually no idea which world he will in fact create, since he does not know how free creatures would act if he created them. All he knows are the possibilities, which are infinite in number. In a sense, what God knows in the logical moment after the decision to create must come as a total surprise to him. He just finds himself with a world and a future. I do not say this idea is impossible, but it is certainly peculiar and diminishes the role of God's wisdom in creation.

Middle knowledge also provides the key to God's providence. Indeed, one of the most helpful consequences of the doctrine of middle knowledge is the reconciliation of divine sovereignty and human freedom. Since God knows what any free creature would do in any situation, he can, by creating the appropriate situations, bring it about that creatures will achieve his ends and purposes and that they will do so *freely*. When one considers that these situations are themselves the results of earlier free decisions by creatures, free decisions which God had to bring about, one begins to see that providence over a world of free creatures could only be the work of omniscience. Only an infinite Mind could calculate the unimaginably complex and numerous factors that would need to be combined in order to bring about through the free decisions of creatures a single human event such as, say, the enactment of the lend-lease policy prior to America's entry into the Second World War. Think then of God's planning the entire course of world history so as to achieve his purposes! Given middle knowledge, the apparent contradiction between God's sovereignty, which seems to crush human freedom, and human freedom, which seems to break God's sovereignty, is resolved. In his infinite intelligence, God is able to plan a world in which his designs are achieved by creatures acting freely. Praise be to God!

Thus, everything which happens comes to pass either by the will or by the permission of God. God wills every good thing directly, and his desire for us is that in whatever circumstances we find ourselves we choose to do good. But he permits sin and allows creatures to do the sinful acts he knew they would do, since he wills creatures to be free. But in his providence God so arranges things that in the end even the sinful acts of creatures will serve to achieve his purposes. As Joseph said to his brothers who had sold him into slavery, "You meant evil against me, but God meant it for good in order to bring about this present result" (Gen. 50:20, New American Standard Bible).

Without middle knowledge, it is difficult to explain divine providence. God could not reason, "If I were to send Christ to

Jerusalem when Pilate is governor, then Pilate would acquiesce to the Jews' demands to have Christ crucified. Therefore, I shall send Christ into those circumstances in order to achieve his expiatory death." Rather, in the moment logically prior to the decision to create, not only would God not know what Pilate would do, but God would also have no idea whatsoever how to bring about the circumstances envisioned. Given the decision to create, God would find himself with only the knowledge, "I shall send Christ to Jerusalem when Pilate is governor, and Pilate will acquiesce to the Jews' demands to have Christ crucified. By this means I shall achieve his expiatory death." But there would be no explanation of why God finds himself with this foreknowledge rather than foreknowledge of some other eventuality. About the only answer that could be given would be, "That's just the way it happens to be."

Finally, middle knowledge provides an intriguing account of predestination, an account which is fully compatible with human freedom. Predestination is just a subcategory of divine providence pertaining to salvation. In the moment of divine middle knowledge, God knew how every possible person in any conceivable circumstance would freely respond to his grace and the drawing of his Spirit. Now the circumstances in which we actually find ourselves include God's gracious initiatives to draw us to himself. God's will is for all to be saved. Therefore, he provides sufficient grace for salvation for each and every person he creates. In his middle knowledge, however, he knows who, as circumstances vary, would freely accept and who would freely reject his initiatives. He knows, for example, under which circumstances Peter would freely accept and under which circumstances he would freely reject God's grace. Accordingly, the very act of selecting a world to be created is a sort of predestination. The persons in that world who God knew would respond most certainly will respond and be saved. Nonetheless, they are still free to reject God's grace. Of course, if they were to reject his grace, God's middle knowledge would have been different. Given that God's middle knowledge is correct, God, in creating certain persons who will freely accept his grace, thereby ensures that they will be saved. As for the unsaved, the only reason they are not predestined is that they freely reject God's grace. God gives sufficient grace to all people everywhere to be saved, and he desires that they accept his grace and be saved; in fact, many of the unsaved may actually receive greater divine assistance and drawing than do the saved. That they are lost is their own responsibility.

Proponents of middle knowledge emphasize that God does not predestine persons because he knows they would receive Christ and persevere. Nor does he select a world because he knows that in it, say, Peter would be saved. Rather, God simply chooses the world he wants, and whoever in that world would freely receive Christ is, by the very act of God's selection of that world, predestined to do so. All the people in that world receive sufficient grace to be among the predestined. Their eternal destiny thus lies in their own hands. Everything depends on whether they freely receive or reject Christ.

Middle knowledge can thus provide an illuminating account not only of God's foreknowledge, but also of his providence and predestination. Does God, then, possess middle knowledge? It would be difficult to prove in any direct way that he does, for the biblical passages are not unequivocal.[1] Nevertheless, the doctrine is so fruitful in illuminating divine prescience, providence, and predestination that it can be presumed unless there are insoluble objections to it.

In fact, it is interesting how often ordinary Christian believers naturally assume that God has middle knowledge. For example, Christians regularly seem to presuppose divine middle knowledge when they pray for God's guidance. They assume that God knows which of two paths would be better for them to take. A girl praying for guidance about two suitors asking for her hand in marriage, for example, might assume that God knows that if she were to marry the one, in the course of time the marriage would go sour, whereas if she were to marry the other, their love would endure and deepen. If God lacks middle knowledge, however, all he can tell the young lady with certainty is what she *will* do, which is no help at all as far as guidance is

---

1. The incident in 1 Samuel 23 could be explained on the basis of God's knowledge of the present character of Saul and the men of Keilah—God could reasonably surmise what they would do if David were to remain. The passage in Matthew 11 is probably religious hyperbole meant merely to underscore the depth of the depravity of the cities in which Jesus preached.

concerned, or else he can advise her simply as a superintelligent but fallible counselor.

Or again, Christians have sometimes espoused middle knowledge when they reflect on the issue of the salvation of infants. One of my former colleagues once remarked that the widely accepted view that persons who die in infancy are all graciously saved by God is untenable because it leads inescapably to the conclusion that the kindest thing that parents can do for their children is to kill them! Instead he proposed that God judges persons who die in infancy on the basis of what they *would* have done if they *had* grown up. Those who would have had faith will be saved, but those who would not have believed will be lost. Similarly, many Christians presume middle knowledge in dealing with the question of the eternal status of those who have never heard about Christ. A training booklet published by the British branch of Campus Crusade for Christ asserts, "God bases his judgement on what would have happened if someone had heard the gospel. It is part of His omniscience to know not only what will happen, but also what would happen if a different set of circumstances were to occur. Jesus states this clearly in Matt. 12:21–23."[2]

Although most of the people who hold views like those we have just described have probably never even so much as heard of middle knowledge, still it is very evident that they are presupposing it. Accepting the doctrine of middle knowledge does not necessarily commit a person to holding such views; on the other hand, these views cannot be held without assuming divine middle knowledge. The assumption, then, that God possesses such knowledge underlies, I think, the views of many ordinary Christians.

Objections to Middle Knowledge

Philosophical Objections

But the doctrine of middle knowledge is, of course, very much a matter of controversy. Two principal philosophical ob-

---

2. Campus Crusade for Christ, Great Britain, "How Can I Turn the Tables in Witnessing?" p. 5.

jections have been lodged against it: (1) counterfactual statements about what a person would have freely done under
different circumstances cannot be true, and (2) such counterfactual statements could not have been known by God in the moment logically prior to his decree to create the world.

According to the first objection, counterfactual statements
about what a person would have freely done under other conditions are without exception either false or else lacking in any
truth value at all. Now on the face of it, such an objection seems
very odd, for we use such statements all the time: "if I had
known you were coming, I would have baked a cake"; "if
Richard Nixon were smarter, he would have destroyed the
tapes"; and so forth. Of course, in many cases we may not *know*
whether such a statement is true—for example, "If FDR had
been healthy at Yalta, he would not have given away the
store"—but our uncertainty or even complete ignorance
provides no reason for thinking that such statements lack any
truth value or are all false. Indeed, sometimes we most certainly
do have a very good idea of whether such counterfactual statements are true. For instance, if I were to offer my wife a plate of
liver and onions and a plate of chocolate-chip cookies, I know
which one she would choose as certainly as I know almost
anything!

In fact, it seems reasonable to suppose that counterfactual
statements of the following form must be either true or false:

> If P were placed in c, then P would choose x (P is any particular
> free person, c is a particular set of circumstances, which includes
> all of past history up to the point of decision, and x is a particular
> action).

To affirm that a statement of this form must be either true or
false is not to affirm that P is determined or forced by the circumstances to choose x or to refrain from choosing x, but to
affirm merely that if placed in such circumstances and left free,
P would either freely choose x or freely refrain from choosing x.
P would not *have* to do either one, but he would have to do one or
the other. If, then, we are to believe that such counterfactual
statements *cannot* be true, the objector must produce an extremely strong argument for this denial.

About the only argument offered for denying that counterfactual statements can be true is that there is no reality to which such statements correspond and therefore they cannot be true, since truth consists in correspondence to reality. Since counterfactual statements are, by definition, contrary to fact, that is, about circumstances and actions which never in fact exist but only *would* exist if things were to be different, they do not correspond to reality and so cannot be true.

This argument seems to rest on the same misconception of truth as correspondence that we considered earlier (pp. 56–58). There we saw that at the time of the truth of future-tense statements, the reality to which they correspond is nonexistent. All that the view of truth as correspondence requires of future-tense statements is that the realities described *will* exist. Similarly, at the time at which counterfactual statements are true, it is not required that the circumstances or actions referred to actually exist. The view of truth as correspondence requires only that such actions *would* be taken if the specified circumstances *were* to exist. Thus, in order for a statement like "if Barry Goldwater had been elected in 1964, he would have won the Vietnam War" to be true, it is not required that Goldwater have been elected president or that the United States have won the war. In order for this statement to be true, it is required only that the United States *would* have won the war *had* Goldwater been elected. Of course, only God knows whether this statement is true or false, but, as was explained above, that is beside the point. The point is that such statements are true if reality *would be* as they describe, given the specified conditions.

It might be objected that while this account suffices for statements about persons who have existed or will exist, it is unsatisfactory for statements about persons who have never existed and never will. For how can a statement like, "if Elvis Presley's sister had gone into singing, she would have been the queen of rock and roll" be true, since Elvis never had a sister? This problem is easily resolved, however, by recalling that in the moment logically prior to the decree to create the world, God knew all possible worlds and all possible persons in those worlds. In some of those worlds in which Elvis exists, he has a sister; indeed, he has different sisters in different worlds. In order to determine whether our statement is true or false, one simply has to be more precise and specify which world and which sister the sentence is referring to. The problem with the sentence as it now stands is that it is too vague; it does not specify P (the person) or c (the circumstances) sufficiently. But once these elements are clearly specified, there seems to be no reason to think that this statement cannot be true, even if whether it is true must remain unknown to us. Hence, it seems to me that what makes counterfactual statements true is the same thing that makes ordinary statements true, namely, correspondence. A statement of the form "if P were placed in c, then P would do x" is true if and only if P would do x if P were placed in c.

But the proponent of middle knowledge is not out of difficulty yet. For contrary to the impression given by some writers, establishing that counterfactual statements about what people would do under different circumstances can be true is not sufficient to establish middle knowledge. For key to the idea of middle knowledge is that such statements are true and known by God at a moment logically prior to his decree to create the world. The second philosophical objection to middle knowledge maintains that even if such statements are now true and known by God posterior to his creative decree, still they could not have been known prior to his decree. Therefore, God lacks middle knowledge.

But why cannot such statements be true and thus known to God prior to his creative decree? The objector, in order to make his case, appeals to the contemporary analysis of what it means for a counterfactual statement to be true or false. According to that analysis, we first consider all possible worlds, as arranged according to their degree of similarity to the actual world. The next step is to pick out those worlds which are most similar to the actual world and in which the antecedent (the "if" clause) of the counterfactual statement is true. To say that the whole counterfactual is true means that in all these worlds the consequent (the "then" clause) is also true. To give an example, the counterfactual statement "if Lyndon Johnson had run for a second term, then he would have been elected" is true if and only if in the possible worlds which are most similar to the actual world and in which it is true that "Johnson runs for a second term," it is also true that "Johnson is elected."

But in the logical moment prior to God's creative decree, the second objection continues, there *is* no actual world yet. For we are talking about a moment before God decrees to create the world; indeed, middle knowledge is supposed to help God decide which world to make actual. But if there is at that moment no actual world yet, statements whose truth value depends on which possible worlds are closest to the actual world cannot be true, for there is as yet no world to be closest to. Therefore, counterfactual statements about what persons would do under different circumstances cannot be true at that point and, hence, cannot be known by God. Only after his decree to create the world can such statements be true, for it is only then that an actual world exists to serve as the reference point to which all possible worlds are to be compared. But then such statements are true too late to serve as God's guides in deciding which world to decree. Thus, God cannot have middle knowledge.

Now at this point the Christian may well feel like responding, "Look, I have good theological grounds for affirming divine middle knowledge, and if current theories concerning the conditions which must be met for counterfactuals to be true cannot accommodate this doctrine, then so much the worse for contemporary theories. The objection serves only to highlight a weakness in these theories." Such a reaction strikes me as entirely justified. Counterfactual statements have been notoriously difficult to analyze, and I feel much more confident of God's possessing middle knowledge than I do of the correctness of the currently fashionable method of analyzing such statements in terms of possible worlds. The latter is, after all, only a proposal, a suggested way of understanding what it means for such statements to be true or false; it cannot be proved like a scientific theory. There could be any number of other ways of analyzing what it means for counterfactual statements to be true. If the current method, which involves identifying the possible worlds most similar to the actual world, cannot make room for divine middle knowledge, then a defender of middle knowledge will simply regard that method as inadequate in this respect and hope that a more suitable theory of counterfactuals will be worked out.

But is the current method really inadequate in this respect? Not at all. The fact is that those who raise the second objection have erred in their understanding of the instantiation of the actual world. For parallel to the three moments in God's knowl-

TABLE 4. **The Logical Order in God's Knowledge and in the Instantiation of the Actual World**

God's Knowledge	Instantiation of the Actual World
1. Natural knowledge	1. Logically necessary states of affairs
2. Middle knowledge	2. Counterfactual states of affairs concerning free decisions of creatures

God's Decision to Create a World	
3. Free knowledge	3. All remaining states of affairs in the actual world

edge there is a sort of logical progression in the instantiation of the actual world. Table 4 correlates the logical order in the instantiation of the actual world with the logical moments in God's knowledge.

In the first moment, which corresponds to God's natural knowledge, those aspects of the world exist which are expressed by logically necessary states of affairs. For example, in this first moment, the state of affairs "$7 + 5 = 12$" is already actual. The state of affairs expressed by this statement is actual, for it is a logical truism, true by definition. So in this first moment, there are many states of the world which are already actual, namely, logically necessary states of affairs, which could not possibly be otherwise.

In the second moment, which corresponds to God's middle knowledge, those aspects of the actual world exist which are states of affairs concerning what free creatures would do in any set of circumstances. For example, in this second moment the state of affairs "if Jones were placed in circumstances c, then he would freely do action x" is actual. Of course, neither Jones nor the circumstances yet exist, except as ideas in God's mind. But it is nevertheless the case that if Jones were to be actualized by God and placed in c, then Jones would freely do x. Thus, the states of affairs which are expressed by true counterfactuals concerning free decisions by humans are in fact already actual at this second moment. So even though at this moment the actual world in all its fullness does not yet exist, nonetheless certain aspects of it already exist, namely, logically necessary states of affairs and states of affairs corresponding to true counterfactuals concerning creaturely freedom.

Finally, in the third moment, after the creative decree of the divine will, all remaining aspects of the actual world exist. For example, the state of affairs "in A.D. 1972 Jones marries his fiancée" is actual. By this third logical moment, the actual world is complete in all its aspects.

Another way of grasping this logically progressive instantiation of the world is to realize that only those states of affairs which depend on God's will for their actualization have to wait for the third moment and the creative decree of the divine will. Those states of affairs which are not so dependent are already actual prior to the decision of the divine will concerning which world to create. Indeed, as we have seen, those already actual states of affairs limit God's options in deciding which world to create: he cannot create a world involving a logical contradiction or a false counterfactual. Thus, for example, it was not open to him to make a world containing square circles or a world in which Peter, if placed in precisely the same circumstances, would not deny Christ.

This understanding of the instantiation of the world undermines the second objection, which is based on the assumption that at the second moment the actual world does not exist. For we have seen that at this moment aspects of the actual world *do* already exist, including states of affairs expressed by certain counterfactuals. Since these counterfactuals correspond to reality, they are at this point true and their opposites false. Since the relevant states of affairs are actual, one can hold to both the doctrine of divine middle knowledge and the current explanation of what it means for a counterfactual to be true: in those possible worlds which are most similar to the actual world (insofar as it exists at the moment) and in which the antecedent is true, the consequent is also true.

It seems, then, that the second objection to middle knowledge fares no better than the first. Indeed, according to Alvin Plantinga, an extremely influential contemporary philosopher of religion who has revived the doctrine of middle knowledge, there simply is no sound philosophical objection to the doctrine of divine middle knowledge.[3]

---

3. Alvin Plantinga, "Reply to Robert Adams," in *Alvin Plantinga*, ed. James Tomberlin and Peter Van Inwagen, Profiles 5 (Dordrecht: D. Reidel, 1985), pp. 378–79.

Now an objector might persist by demanding to know the basis of divine middle knowledge. How does God know what any possible person would do under any possible set of circumstances? But here it seems to me that the two answers given by the Jesuit theologians are basically satisfactory. Why could one not maintain that God, in virtue of his exhaustive knowledge of every single possible person, so that he discerns even what we would freely do in any circumstance in which he might place us, knows which counterfactuals concerning human freedom are true? I know my wife well enough to know what she would freely do under certain circumstances (recall the liver and onions). So why could not God know us so completely that he knows what we would freely do under any circumstances? I do not think that this solution leads to any sort of "character determinism," for when I say my wife would choose the chocolate-chip cookies over the liver and onions, I in no way think that her choice is *determined*; rather, she freely makes such a decision.

If this solution should prove unacceptable, however, one could point instead to God's innate knowledge. God has the essential property of knowing all truth; certain counterfactuals are true; therefore. . . . We have already seen that this solution can be employed to account for divine foreknowledge: there is no reason it cannot be pushed back a notch and used here instead. Neither of these two solutions seems impossible, and that is all the defender of middle knowledge has to show.

Theological Objections

But if there is no cogent philosophical objection to divine middle knowledge, perhaps it is theologically objectionable. One might argue, for example, that it is impossible, given such a doctrine, to explain why God, if he desires all people to be saved, should create a world in which so many people are lost and eternally damned. For by his middle knowledge, God knew under what circumstances any person he might create would freely receive Christ. So why did he not plan his creation of persons and circumstances in such a way that everyone would freely be saved? The opponents of middle knowledge face no such problem because, in their view, in the logical moment prior to creation God had no idea how many would be saved and how many lost, indeed, whether human beings would fall into sin or whether Christ would have to come (unless, of course, it is held that God decreed all these things himself). Once he created the world and found out how many were actually being lost, God might even have regretted his action. Those of us who hold that God has middle knowledge and really does want everyone to be saved, however, face the difficulty of trying to explain the fact that so many are lost.

Now a little reflection reveals that the objector is really claiming that it is impossible to believe consistently the following four statements:

1. God has middle knowledge.
2. God is omnipotent.
3. God is all-loving.
4. Some persons freely reject Christ and are lost.

The objector claims that if we believe the first three statements, then we cannot accept the fourth statement. But since the fourth statement is cerainly true, it follows that we have to reject one of the first three instead. Christians cannot reject the second or third statements; therefore, we must reject the first and deny that God has middle knowledge.

But is it impossible to believe consistently all four statements? There is no *explicit* contradiction between them. For none of the statements is the negation of any of the others. The objector must rather be saying that there is an *implicit* contradiction between these statements. But how is that to be shown?

The objector might claim that the Christian who accepts statements (1)–(3) ought also to accept as necessarily true the following three related statements:

1'. God knows under what circumstances any possible person would freely receive Christ.
2'. God is able to create a world in which all persons freely receive Christ.
3'. God holds that a world in which nobody rejects Christ is preferable to a world in which somebody does and consequently is lost.

From statements (1')–(3') the objector might argue that it is impossible that God should create a world in which some persons freely reject Christ and are lost. For he prefers a world in which no one is lost, and he has the knowledge and power to bring about such a world. Therefore, if he chooses to create a world it must be one in which everyone is saved—otherwise, God is lacking in knowledge, power, or love.

But the problem with this argument is that statements (1')–(3') are not necessarily true. Indeed, I suspect that at least two of them are false. To begin with (1'), it is possible, on the contrary, that the following is true:

> 1". There are some possible persons who would not freely receive Christ under any circumstances.

In other words, some people, no matter how much the Spirit of God worked on their hearts, no matter how favorable their upbringing, no matter how many times or ways they heard the gospel, would still refuse to bow the knee and give their lives to Christ. Not only is (1") possibly true, but I believe that it probably is in fact true. But then God cannot create a world in which such persons freely receive Christ and are saved. Only if God coerced them would they believe in Christ; hence, God cannot be blamed for creating a world in which such people are lost.

The objector might retort, "But why doesn't God just refrain from creating any of these people? He could create a world of *other* people under circumstances in which they would freely receive Christ." But contrary to this response, which is in essence equivalent to statement (2'), it is possible that the following is true:

> 2". There is no possible world in which all persons would freely receive Christ.

In other words, it is possible that no matter what world God created, someone would be stiff-necked and refuse to believe in Christ. This seems the more probable the more persons God creates. Hence, it is possible that God is not, after all, able to create a world in which all persons freely receive Christ.

The objector might protest that God could have created a world in which only a few persons existed (or perhaps even only one) and that all such persons would have received Christ freely. But at this point I think we ought to call (3′) into question. It is at least possible (and I think very probably true) that God would prefer to create a world in which many people are saved and a few lost than to create a world in which a handful of people are saved and nobody lost. That is to say, the following is possibly true:

   3″. God holds that a world in which some persons freely reject Christ but the number of those who freely receive him is maximized is preferable to a world in which a few people receive Christ and none are lost.

In other words, God may be willing, for the sake of those who are to be saved, to permit the existence of other persons who freely reject his grace and are lost. It may be that the cost of having a certain number of elect is having a certain number of lost.

The objector's argument thus seems questionable at every step. The objection to middle knowledge fails to show that it is necessarily true that God knows under what circumstances any person would freely receive Christ, that God is able to create a world in which all persons freely receive Christ, and that God prefers a world in which no one rejects Christ to a world in which somebody does. As long as the opposites of these statements are even *possible*, the attempt to show that middle knowledge, omnipotence, and omnibenevolence are incompatible with persons' being lost must fail. It is therefore entirely consistent to believe the original statements (1)–(4).

But we can go even further. Not only can we refute the objector's claim that statements (1)–(4) are inconsistent, but we can actually prove that they are consistent. All we have to do is come up with a fifth statement that is consistent with (1)–(3) and that together with them entails (4).

We have seen that it is possible that God wants to maximize the number of the saved. He wants heaven to be as full as possible. Yet as a loving God he wants to minimize the number of the lost. He wants hell to be as empty as possible. His goal, then, is to achieve an optimal balance, to create no more lost than is necessary to actualize a certain number of the saved. But it is possible that the balance in the actual world is such an optimal balance. It is possible that in order to create the number of persons in our world who will be saved, God had to create the number of persons who will be lost. It is possible that the terrible price of filling heaven is the filling of hell as well, and that in any other possible world the balance between saved and lost would have been worse or the same. It is possible that had God created a world with fewer persons in hell, there would be fewer persons in heaven. It is possible that in order to achieve this much blessedness, God was forced to put up with this much loss. Even if God could have achieved a better ratio between saved and lost, it is possible that in order to better the ratio between them, God would have had to reduce the number of the saved so drastically as to leave heaven deficient in population (say, by creating a world of only four people, three of whom would go to heaven and one to hell). It is possible that in order to achieve a multitude of saints, God had to accept an even greater multitude of sinners.

It might be protested that necessarily a loving God would not create so many persons who will be actually lost, but who would under different circumstances have been saved. A loving God could not, in order to achieve one person's salvation, allow other people to be created and lost who would themselves under other circumstances have been saved.[4] However, we have seen that it is possible that some persons would never receive Christ under any circumstances. Suppose, then, that God has so ordered the

---

4. I shall assume that this is true. But some might disagree, arguing that as long as God provides to all people sufficient grace for salvation and those who are lost are such because they freely reject God's grace, then God cannot be called unloving because he did not give them more grace. D. A. Carson comments, "Three large theological propositions are presupposed by Jesus' insistence that . . . things will go worse for the cities that have received so much light than for the pagan cities. The first is that the Judge has contingent knowledge: he knows what Tyre and Sidon would have done under such-and-such circumstances. The second is that God does not owe revelation to anyone, or else there is injustice in withholding it. The third is that punishment on the Day of Judgment takes into account opportunity. There are degrees of felicity in paradise and degrees of torment in hell. . . . The implications for Western, English-speaking Christendom today are sobering" (*Matthew*, Expositor's Bible Commentary 8 [Grand Rapids: Zondervan, 1984], p. 273).

world that all those persons who are actually lost are such persons. That is to say, suppose that those persons who actually go to hell would have gone to hell no matter what world they were created in. It is possible that all who are lost would have been lost in any world in which God actualized them. It is possible, then, that in order to bring as many people to salvation as he has, God has to pay the price of the number of people who are lost, but that he has providentially ordered things in such a way that those who are lost are those who would never have been saved in any case.

At this point, then, we can construct a statement that is consistent with (1)–(3) and that together with them entails (4):

5. The actual world contains an optimal balance between saved and unsaved, and those who are unsaved would never have received Christ under any circumstances.

Notice that in order to show that statements (1)–(4) are consistent, (5) does not need to be true—all it needs to be is *possibly* true. That is enough to show that the four original statements are consistent. As long as (5) is possible—and it certainly seems to be—then one is entirely consistent in believing statements (1)–(4).

One is thus able to believe consistently that God has middle knowledge, that God is omnipotent, that God is all-loving, and yet that some persons freely reject Christ and are forever lost. For it is possible that the actual world has an optimal balance between saved and unsaved and that those who are lost would not have freely believed in Christ under any circumstances.

This solution to the theological objection to middle knowledge also serves, by the way, to illuminate the old problem of the fate of those who never hear the gospel. However God judges them, it might be claimed that an all-loving God could not send people to hell for rejecting the light that they had (general revelation in nature, for example), if he knows that they would have received Christ if only they had heard of him. An all-loving God would make sure that the light of the gospel, to which he knows they would respond, would reach such persons. The reader will undoubtedly have surmised the way out of this dilemma: it is possible that God in his providence so arranged the world that those who never in fact hear the gospel are persons who would not respond to it if they did hear it. God brings the gospel to all those who he knows will respond to it if they hear it. Thus the motivation for the missionary enterprise is to be God's ambassadors in bringing the gospel to those whom God has arranged to freely receive it when they hear it. No one who would respond if he heard it will be lost.

Hence not only does there appear to be no good philosophical objection to middle knowledge, but there also seems to be no good theological objection either. It is possible for God to have middle knowledge, to be omnipotent, and to genuinely desire that everyone be saved, and yet for some persons to be lost. God is a loving God and therefore supplies sufficient grace for salvation to all persons, even to those he knows will reject it. That many individuals are lost is therefore the result of the free choice of their own will. God cannot be blamed for their damnation.

We have seen that the doctrine of divine middle knowledge, while having some biblical support, ought to be accepted mainly because of its great theological advantages. It provides a basis for God's foreknowledge of the future free acts of individuals. It furnishes an insightful and exciting account of God's providence and of the relation between divine sovereignty and human freedom. And it may be helpful in understanding the biblical doctrine of predestination. Philosophical objections based on the view of truth as correspondence and on the current interpretation of what it means for a counterfactual statement to be true were seen to embody misunderstandings; once these are cleared up the objections vanish. Theologically, it is entirely consistent to hold to middle knowledge and the traditional concept of God and to the fact that many persons will not be saved. Indeed, the doctrine of middle knowledge may illuminate the difficult question regarding the reason some persons are lost and the fate of those who never hear of Christ. For these reasons, I am an enthusiastic supporter of the doctrine of middle knowledge and find it one of the most intriguing and comforting aspects of divine omniscience.

Suggested Further Reading

Molina, Luis. *Molina on Foreknowledge: Part IV of Luis Molina's "Concordia."* Translated and edited by Alfred J. Freddoso. Forthcoming.

Lewis, David. *Counterfactuals.* Oxford: Clarendon, 1974.

Plantinga, Alvin. *The Nature of Necessity.* Oxford: Clarendon, 1974. See pp. 169–80.

Adams, Robert. "Middle Knowledge and the Problem of Evil." *American Philosophical Quarterly* 14 (1977): 109–17.

Plantinga, Alvin. "Reply to Robert Adams." In *Alvin Plantinga*, edited by James Tomberlin and Peter Van Inwagen, pp. 371–82. Profiles 5. Dordrecht: D. Reidel, 1985.

Flint, Thomas P. "The Problem of Divine Freedom." *American Philosophical Quarterly* 20 (1983): 225–64.

———, and Alfred J. Freddoso. "Maximal Power." In *The Existence and Nature of God*, edited by Alfred J. Freddoso, pp. 81–113. Notre Dame, Ind.: University of Notre Dame Press, 1983.

Epilogue

C. H. Spurgeon once remarked,

> The proper study of a Christian is the Godhead. The highest science, the loftiest speculation, the mightiest philosophy, which can ever engage the attention of a child of God, is the name, the nature, the person, the work, the doings, and the existence of the great God whom he calls his Father.
>
> There is something exceedingly *improving to the mind* in a contemplation of the Divinity. It is a subject so vast, that all our thoughts are lost in its immensity; so deep, that our pride is drowned in its infinity. . . . No subject of contemplation will tend more to humble the mind, than thoughts of God. . . .
>
> But while the subject *humbles* the mind, it also *expands* it. He who often thinks of God, will have a larger mind than the man who simply plods around this narrow globe. . . . Nothing will so enlarge the intellect, nothing so magnify the whole soul of man, as a devout, earnest, continued investigation of the great subject of the Deity.[1]

I hope that the reader of this book has sensed both the awe and exhilaration of which Spurgeon spoke. I have found that the more I reflect philosophically on the attributes of God, the more overwhelmed I become at his greatness and the more excited I become about Bible doctrine. Whereas easy appeals to mystery prematurely shut off reflection about God, rigorous and earnest

---

1. C. H. Spurgeon, quoted in J. I. Packer, *Knowing God* (London: Hodder & Stoughton, 1973), pp. 13–14.

effort to understand him is richly rewarded with deeper appreciation of who he is, more confidence in his reality and care, and a more intelligent and profound worship of his person.

With particular regard to the attribute of omniscience, we have seen that the Bible teaches that God knows completely not only the past and present, but also the future, including the free acts of individuals. Neither the attempt to deny divine foreknowledge nor the attempt to deny human freedom can make its peace with the biblical text. This fact at once raises the question as to whether divine foreknowledge and human freedom are compatible. We have seen that attempts to demonstrate that they are incompatible are logically fallacious or entail erroneous notions of the necessity of the past. Moreover, research into parallel topics like backward causation, time travel, precognition, and Newcomb's paradox has similarly exposed and rejected fatalistic reasoning. The right-thinking theologian ought, therefore, also to reject such reasoning in the province of theology. Divine foreknowledge and human freedom seem entirely compatible.

But if divine foreknowledge and human freedom are compatible, it still might be objected that God has no basis for knowing future free acts. This objection, however, fails to disprove the possibility that God may have either an innate knowledge of all true future-tense statements or middle knowledge as a basis of his knowledge of the actual future. These possible solutions not only show that God can indeed have good basis for his beliefs about the future, but also illuminate other areas of Christian doctrine as well.

"O the depth of the riches and wisdom and knowledge of God!" (Rom. 11:33). We can only stand in awe of this infinite Mind, this incredibly vast and complex Intelligence, who arranged and decreed a universe of creatures moving certainly toward his previsioned ends by their own free choices, who knows the end from the beginning, and who loves us and wills our eternal salvation. "To the only wise God be glory for evermore through Jesus Christ!" (Rom. 16:27).

Index

155

Made in the USA
Columbia, SC
29 July 2020